THE ESCAPE FROM EDEN

The Texas Republic Series

THE ESCAPE FROM EDEN

The Texas Republic Series

JOE L. BLEVINS

Order this book online at www.trafford.com
or email orders@trafford.com

Most Trafford titles are also available at major online book retailers.

Illustrations by Joe L. Blevins

Printed in the United States of America.

ISBN: 978-1-4269-4806-0 (sc)
ISBN: 978-1-4269-4807-7 (hc)
ISBN: 978-1-4269-4808-4 (e)

Library of Congress Control Number: 2010916837

Trafford rev. 12/13/2010

 www.trafford.com

North America & international
toll-free: 1 888 232 4444 (USA & Canada)
phone: 250 383 6864 ◆ fax: 812 355 4082

THE ESCAPE FROM EDEN

This book is based on true historical accounts
by following an accurate time line.

Based on the Texas Republic 1836-1845
Original Copyright 2001
Revised and New Edited Versions
Joe L. Blevins

To John Wesley Blevins, my twin brother.

(From 01-21-1956 to 12-02-1997.)

You inspired me to finish this work.

PREFACE

The Escape from Eden tells the story of Andrew: a freedman from Baton Rouge Louisiana. Freedmen were often indentured servants from all races and creeds as many people had their debts bought off by others that were well off. After seven years of working off a debt a person was declared free. Andrew was an African American. He learned to read by copying the alphabet from an old Bible he found. He started writing a journal to keep track of the crops he raised. In time it told of the events in his life. Andrew wrote about his freedom and his move to Texas when smugglers took his home as a hideout.

Andrew tells of his trip to Nacogdoches to meet with Sam Houston, a lawyer, and the leader of the Texas army. Andrew signs up for the land grants in east Texas. He must serve two years as a soldier to get his land grant. He must see if a freedman can own land in Texas. There was a dispute pending in the Nacogdoches over William Goyens' water rights. Circuit judge Ellis B. Thomas held a hearing for Goyens, who was a freedman that was a businessman that owned a livery stable, a hotel, mercantile store, and a saloon.

Andrew's case was passed because he has a manumission letter stating that he 'belongs to himself and God.' Sam Houston now represents Andrew and his wife Delephine. He wins the right to serve in the Texas army and get a land grant and a map of the land grants in east Texas. Sam Houston gives him four weeks to put up a cabin since winter is soon to come. He is then to report to Nacogdoches for military duty. On his way to the land grant he is attacked by robbers. Delephine is killed. Andrew is badly wounded. He hides in some brush until daylight. Some Cherokee on a hunting party find him close to death. They save him and bring him to their village. William Goyens comes to the Cherokee camp to trade horses. He meets Andrew again. He explains to Andrew that the Cherokee want him as a part of their tribe. The Mexican army invades into east Texas to take horses and cattle. General Sam Houston asks the Cherokee to act as scouts for the Texas army. Andrew is in the army as a scout. His new wife Say-te-Qua and family make him determined to protect his home from raids of the Mexican army. His faith in God pulls Andrew through the tough times ahead. His path leads him into the heat of the San Jacinto battle: the quest for Texas Independence. Each time you read the Escape from Eden you will learn of the people and events that made Texas great.

Joe L. Blevins.

ABOUT THE AUTHOR:

Joe L. Blevins is an artist and writer. Joe is the author of six books. He has a great love of Texan and American history. He started drawing at the early age. A lady at church gave him a little paint set and some drawing paper. For fifty years it has been a learning experience. Joe drew the animals that he saw in the pastures. He drew the faces of the Indians that he knew of. This was to help tell the story by putting a "face" on history. Since the Native Americans are the earliest culture here Joe wanted to show his deep respect and love for their culture. Joe's family was some of the earliest Peter's Colonists to come to the Dove Creek at a place called Cross Timbers. They helped set up the earliest church in that area called Lonesome Dove Church. It was the earliest planned settlement and church. His paternal grandmother Rosa Lee Torian was born in the Torian log cabin along Dove Creek. It was moved in 1974 to the Grapevine Town Square as a Texas' Historical Place as the oldest building in Tarrant County. His paternal grandfather Lesley Green Blevins was born in the Choctaw nation of Indian Territory in 1889. He moved to Texas when Oklahoma became a state. He was a justice of the peace in Grapevine during the 1950's. His stories are the inspiration for this book.

Joe grew up in Grapevine where true stories of the early Texan pioneers were told by his close family. It was a long standing tradition to pass down the family history. He is related to Peter's Colonists that settled Texas when it was still a republic. These books represents many years of study and research on his part. Joe heard about Sam Houston and the 1843 Red Bird Treaty growing up as it happened in the early history of his hometown. This treaty ended a three year Indian war so that new settlements could continue in Texas. It was these stories that Joe found so interesting. He wanted to organize them and write them down for other people to enjoy. These true stories still ring true over time. Putting these stories together was a joy. Factual stories and real characters from early Texas are found here. Why read fictional stories when factual stories are more interesting?! Joe writes here in the context of the 19th century times and word usage. These words are written the way Andrew actually spoke. People in those days did not have an education in a school. They were self-taught. They had common sense, so they knew much about living a good and decent life.

Joe L. Blevins The Escape From Eden.

TABLE OF CONTENTS

CHAPTER ONE

Our Life in Louisiana

A young woman went to an auction with her husband. They hoped to find something unusual and unexpected. She first looked in the auction catalog beforehand to get an idea of what she could afford. The thing that caught her attention was an old stagecoach trunk that could be redone and made into a nice piece of furniture for the den. "Most of the items are out of my price range, but here is one that I could bid on," she thought. The bidding began. The most expensive items came and went. It was close to the end of the auction. Her item was number 50. She is the only bidder, "forty-five dollars!" the auctioneer said. She is delighted with her new prize. She is excited to get home so she can investigate the items inside the trunk. She comes home and carefully unwrapped all the items from the brown paper wrappers.

Inside the trunk are some old saddlebags, a worn Bible, and some journals full of writing and drawings. She then found a small tobacco pouch made of leather, with beadwork on it. Inside of it is a silver dollar dated 1834. The woman looked at the old Bible's cover. Inside the pages are records of births, baptisms, weddings, and deaths. Many verses are underlined. Bookmarks are set at their favorite passages. In the back of the Bible is a legal letter that is signed and notarized by two lawyers and a judge. The old envelope reads, "Manumission Letter, 1834". It states: "Since the bearer is a freeman he owes no debts, so he is free to move about, as any man. He belongs to himself and God." This interests her to look at the first journal, so she begins to read out loud to her husband.

The first entry in the diary starts: May 12, 1834. "This book belongs to Andrew. We now live on the Bayou Pierre close to Flatwoods Louisiana. We abide by the "Golden Rule" here. Delephine and I work for an elderly man named Mister Jeremy Mack Guffey. He is like our own father: a fair-minded man past sixty years old. He works out in the fields as hard as any man twenty years younger! He has no children of his own. His wife Anna died in childbirth over twenty years ago. He never married again. Soon after that time we are brought here to live. Mister Jeremy was at an auction to buy horses. He entered a slave auction by mistake. He was appalled at what he saw there, so he stole us away when he saw a chance.

He ran some horses through the slave auction. He took us away as the crowd scattered. We found a canoe hidden in the rushes. We stole away down the Mississippi River to the Red River. For many days we traveled until we could no longer hear the dogs and hired soldiers tracking us. We have lived here since then farming, and tending to all the animals. We work here as partners more than any servants. Mister Jeremy said that he saved us from terrible people at Baton Rouge. It was at the great risk of death to us all if we got caught. He took us far from them as he moved from Alexandria to Flatwoods. We hide safely because only gunrunners and smugglers live along the Arroyo Hondo and the Bayou Pierre. We are secure living here. Even the Federal army is afraid to come here because of the quicksand, the alligators, and the Typhoid. The Sabine River trade has brought gunrunners, mercenaries, outlaws, river pirates and worse characters. No one bothers us too much because we are poor and modest people. We have nothing of value other than our own lives. Our home is a four-room cabin made of cedar logs with new wood shingles. We have our own room on the eastern side of the house. The southern room is where we spend most of our time stringing beans, or eating something good that we just hunted. We cook over the stone fireplace. We boil water to drink when the well goes dry. We are comfortable and warm at night. It is a tough life here, but we are more fortunate than most folks. We have the security of being a family. That is all we need. We live by our faith as this is tough as any armor, or weapon.

Today we planted eight acres of wheat. The last two weeks we plowed up all the new fields. The sun was so strong on the back of our necks. We mixed the wheat seeds with sand to make the seed go evenly out of the can that spreads the seed as we drive the harrow over this clay dirt. It stays wet here long enough to let the wheat mature, but not too wet. By the time we get the horses and tack put up the evening stars are out. We eat a late dinner and we will sleep like logs until the cock's crow. Morning always comes early, before we know it. There is too much to do and little time to rest tonight.

Tonight we read ROMANS, Chapter 13, verse 9, "The Golden Rule."

May 16, 1834. We got 4 new workhorses and a new milk cow at the Pineville auction. Mister Jeremy was gone to buy a new rifle so I wrote out a proper bill of sale the best that I could. Only to find that the man I traded with could not read his own name! I did not think that he could not read, or add at all. I read out the details of the sale to his satisfaction.

The auctioneer witnessed this with all the proper signatures. Delephine thought it was all chicken scratches on paper as far as she was concerned. I will teach her to read. I keep on practicing as I have to so I will read and write much better. I will not show too many people outside my household until I feel that I can write. I write here to help improve my worth. Mr. Jeremy would not mind for I could be a big help by keeping track of things. I read the Bible out loud after the chores were done. It is the only book we have. We are more fortunate than most folks living here since we have a place to sleep and enough to eat. Reading and writing keeps my mind sharp and my heart feeling strong. We have little as far as luxury, but we have just what we need. We are great in our love and concern for each other. This is all a family needs. I remember this text from the Bible, the best.

Galatians Chapter 4, verses 4-7. "But when the fullness of time was come, God sent forth His Son, made of a woman, made under the law. To redeem them that were under the law, that we might receive the adoption as sons. And because ye are sons, God hath sent forth the Spirit of His Son into your hearts, crying Abba! Father! Wherefore thou art no more a servant, but a son: and if a son, then an heir of God through Jesus Christ.

July 18, 1834. It is early in the morning, well before five. Some strong coffee is in order. The iron stove is warming up nicely from the cedar wood burning. We place a small cedar log next to a bigger oak log to start a good backfire to cook on. We eat beans, beans, and more pinto beans. It is all good.

We have some cabbage and corn pone. We threw in two stalks of collard greens that Delephine carefully washes before she cooks it. She knows I don't like tallow bugs floating in my greens. I do not like them all gritty tasting either. Our hard work all day merits a good, hearty meal. We eat like it is our last meal: as it just might be one day soon. We work like there is not tomorrow so often we eat good as there is often little time to rest or stop to eat at a regular time.

We say our prayers before we eat and go to sleep at night. A year ago a woman missionary named Ruth Ann Bates witnessed to us from the Bible. She read us John chapter three, and Romans chapter three and verse twenty three. We accepted Jesus Christ. Each of us was baptized in the Cane River. I bought us a new Bible for giving a silver dollar. The old Bible we found years ago was just falling apart. Mister Jeremy would read to us the Scriptures after the day's work is done. I have picked out a few words over time until I could read whole verses. We spent our night times talking about what we read. Mister Jeremy's eyes are not so good after spending too many hot summers in the Louisiana sun. He has trouble reading a month old newspaper. "They are making the print smaller. I don't know why!" The print is just hard for him to see these days. He said that we are over due to learn how to read and write. Our home is dry and clean with a red clay dirt floor. Mister Jeremy drew the letters in the dirt with a pointed cane switch I cut for him. We practiced all our letters, and numbers. Delephine can now write out her name better. This week of rain gave us the time to be indoors to practice our letters, and numbers better. It is too wet to work outside, so we felt it is a good thing for us all to learn to better read and write. The second week we are trying to help Delephine read some favorite Bible passages. After work tonight I read the Third Chapter of John. It was exciting for her to hear the words, to really know what it means. Mister Jeremy is pleased that our learning is so helpful to him. He said that we would get some big carpenter's pencils and white butcher paper to write on the next trip into town. We all lean to help as much as we can since there are so few helpers with so much to do every day.

July 22. Tonight an old peddler came here to get out of the pouring rain. I asked him about the latest news. He told us what he knew about the trade dollar and the high prices for new goods these days. He said that the trade days at Shreveport are so big that they had to burn off more fields to hold all the people and tents that are put up. People are putting up barter for goods since money is so scarce. Everything from chickens to horses is taking the place of money for trade. The peddler told us about the arriving ships to New Orleans that had to be burned. Most of the Irish passengers were ill or close to death. We hated to hear about that and I am sorry that I asked. He politely asked us to stay the night in the barn. I took his horse and bedded it down. He can stay as long as he did not turn over the lantern. Mister Jeremy allowed him to stay and avoid the flood that came down so strong. The peddler gave us three blank journals, some black India ink, and some good quill pens to write with! Now we can make notes on all our crops, and keep a better count of our cattle and horses. The peddler had a little mule and a goat for sale. We bought the little mule to put in with the calves to help keep the wolves and dogs away. He asked two dollars for the goat. Since his travel was hindered by it he made us a good deal. Father nodded that he approved of the deal. We had him sign and date the bill of sale. His last name was Poushay. I put the bill of sale inside the front cover of the journal to keep it from being lost. This can keep a rope away from your neck. People have been quick to hang someone lately, with all the stealing going on. The man gave us a recent newspaper and we were happy to read it. We gave him some boiled eggs, some wheat bread and some goat cheese. Delephine gave him some stout coffee and a dry horse blanket. He was happy to be out of the storm, and we enjoy getting some company to visit and tell us the latest news. He left the next morning after the Cane River crested. The river soon receded and it left driftwood high into the cottonwood trees.

August 26, 1834. All the rain and our hard work have paid off. The wheat is full with the heads so heavy. It will be ready to harvest soon. We get all the long handled sickles sharpened with corn oil and a tan Arkansas sharpening stone. The sickles and scythes are sharp enough to shave a sheep with. Today we will go out early and start cutting and stacking the wheat. We make much good progress today. Delephine cut the twine plenty long this time. She kept us supplied with some cool water to drink. This morning she put a cantaloupe in a bucket then placed it down the well. It was so cold when she peeled it and brought it to us. I felt renewed after a few slices. She took over our place to help take up the slack when we stopped to drink water and rest a few moments. She offered to have dinner ready but we had too much to do and so little time to do everything. We have five more bushels of wheat per acre this year! This means that our careful planning and labor is finally paying off. We lay out a canvas tent flat on the ground for a good threshing floor. Mister Jeremy was working up a storm stacking the bundles of wheat in the wagon. We stopped cutting the stalks directly and helped him stack some bundles. We have much wheat straw left over to make nice brooms to sell later this year.

It is hard to complete this full week of harvest. Mister Jeremy said that we would all prosper greatly from the sale of the wheat. Prices for flour are higher so we are to share in this profit together. It made the burden of the work not so bad. We laid down a canvas tent on the ground as I got our wheat stacked, and threshed by throwing it on the threshing floor. We then picked up the canvas tent and poured the wheat grains into our deepest wagon. We then covered the grain with the same canvas to keep the rain and wind out. We will go to the flourmill at Natchitoches. The stores at Shreveport and Jefferson always give us a good price for our crops. We figured that this year will give us a bonus of forty dollars each to buy something for ourselves. We each talked about what we would buy if given the chance. We will go there in early September, over a week away. We will travel and get some time to visit the Shreveport trade market for a few days.

August 28. Some poor women stopped to get the grain we left on the edges of the fields. Mister Jeremy told us to always welcome them as they are in need as times have been tough. It has left people without something decent for the table. Many men have left to find their way to work in a different state. Some have not come back home. We took the widows some grapevine baskets to fill up to help them gather enough for the next month. They offer to sew and darn things for us, but we do not expect any pay. One is a widow named Lalaurie who is a good seamstress. Times are hard so few can buy new clothes these days. They took the baskets and filled them up good. We told them to come back to get more if they want it. Mister Jeremy said that the widows and orphans are always welcome to glean what they want from the fields after the harvest is finished to fill their own food pantries. We took the widows a bucket of cool water, a basket of okra, some ripe jujus, and some fresh eggs. Delephine took them a few shirts and breeches to mend, so they were happy to have something to do. We have over half a bolt of good cloth that they can have to make something for themselves or their family. It was more that they enjoyed giving us something back and feeling useful to us in return. Our father was proud to see us helping those less fortunate. We do not have much, but there are others who have much less than us. The shoe could always be on the other foot as we are always a stop short of trouble here. We are good people here that want a better life and a future. A good neighbor always wants to help out when they can.

We now have twenty rows of okra to trade. We cut the smallest and tender to eat. We cut the okra early to keep the itch from being so bad. Our long-sleeved shirt protects us from being scratched up. The past 2 days we got 10 bushels to trade for. The hot summer, and the long days of sun have made us profit. We have a big pot of gumbo with a nice possum dressed out good.

Tonight, we read the Bible after we work. We just open up the Bible and read where ever we turn to. Tonight we read the book of Exodus about Moses, who freed the Jews from the bondage of slavery. This king of Egypt was the pharaoh: a great king over North Africa. His land covered over some conquered kings. We then wondered about what our life would be like if Mister Jeremy had not taken us from the terrible slave traders at Baton Rouge. We live here as good as any family can. We will choose to prosper here. The Lord has blessed us very well to live on the Bayou Pierre. The poor are always among us, but we live as well as we can. We have just what we need and nothing more. It makes us grateful for what little we do get.

September 18, 1834. We set about to get all our things ready to go to Shreveport to buy the things that we will need for the winter. We get everything ready to take with us tomorrow morning. Mister Jeremy called out loud for us to hurry into his room. We find Mister Jeremy quite ill from a high fever. His skin has red blotches across his cheeks. He seemed a bit more anxious than usual, but he is a strong, proud man. He opened his eyes wide and fussed that Delephine was burning the biscuits. We took out the cure bag to find something good for a fever. We found the marshmallow, some mesquite leaves for tea, some willow bark for pain, or the garlics in a beef broth. We then best kept him cool from the block of ice that we chipped from the pond last winter. Our storeroom is kept cool by it. We figured that some linens soaked with pieces of that ice would save him.

His fever stays high for over two days. We keep him soaked with ice chips and water. He kept talking out of his head due to the high fever. He said, "There is a letter in the dresser, top drawer. Please get it." So we looked as he requested. I found a large white envelope to bring it to him. He said that we should open it to read it all back for him. We brought him some water to drink. He then asked for a stout cup of coffee. She poured a bit of moonshine in there as it is good as a medicine in some cases. Delephine fixed him his coffee then his color looked a bit better. His eyes opened up wider. He drank it down good and he wanted some more. He is more alert than he has been in some days. He is fussing about reading the letters, so we do. He says that a while back in Natchitoches he asked his lawyer and his associate to be witness to his will, and his final wishes. We don't want to hear these words because we want our father to be well. He insists to be heard so we had better listen to him. The will says that upon his death that we are to be declared free for the rest of our lives. "No one can own us, or buy us, because we belong to ourselves and God." No one can say we owe them any debts. We are not to be anyone's new slaves or do we have to live in a debtor's prison! This was the best news to us. Still it was a small consolation. Mister Jeremy has always treated us like his own family. After losing his wife and son he realized how precious life is. He told us so many times. So when he saw us at the slave auction he had mercy on us as small children. Life is too short and so is our time is here, together. He told us that this land would become ours: for keeps. He always called this place his "Little Eden": a small piece of Paradise. All his long outstanding debts are now paid in full. So if anyone makes claims against us, then they are in the wrong. All his possessions are ours, free and clear to do with as we wish. We may stay here, or we may sell it all to use for our old age. The important thing is that we own it free and clear, and no one can claim it away from us! We are to remain free, and none can put us in a dirty debtor's prison! We would rather stay here with Mister Jeremy by farming our 'Little Eden'. We could enjoy the fruits of our hard work. This is the only life that we know. We work and we farm to harvest the fields together, as a family. Apart we are weak and useless.

This evening we all sat together. Father talked with us about his wishes and concerns. We got sad about all this. Mister Jeremy fussed at us. He does not want any tears but that we celebrate our good lives spent well together. He told us that we are like his own children. We always have been from the start. Delephine and I each held his hand as we kneeled down to pray for him. Some long time has passed. He touched the top of both our heads for us to sit and talk with him. We wrote down all of his concerns to make certain we follow his will. We promised to do our very best to prosper here. Mister Jeremy asked me to read from the Bible. He got much comfort at our day together. He said, "We are 'Making Plans'." We acted brave as he gets mad if we ever feel sorry for him. He scolded us to make us mind: like a good father does. We then let Mister Jeremy rest as he is quite tired. We give him more water to drink to make him comfortable. Delephine put a cool rag over his forehead and eyes. We both prayed for our father. We sat in the chairs by the bed just in case he needs us. We finally slept for the first time in a long while.

We woke the next morning to find that our father has passed away! For almost a day we cried and prayed. We are just beside ourselves for we know not what to do. The animals went unattended for the first time in memory. A big storm came as we huddled together as the lightning flashed and the rain came down hard. Part of the roof came off but we have bigger problems. We stayed beside father's bed to cry until we could not cry anymore. We prayed until the words would no longer come out. I think we both passed out from being so tired from it all. It was most terrible, but father would want us to be strong.

September 24. A man came and knocked on the door for the longest time. We finally answered the door and he saw that we are in mourning. Mister Harris has come to buy a horse that was posted for sale at the gristmill a while back. He apologized for coming at such a bad time. We just gave him the black horse he asked for. In payment we asked him to pass along the word about Mister Jeremy passing away as he traveled on. He sent word to the constable at Pineville. The preacher and several wagons of men, women, and children arrived in late afternoon for his wake. Members of the farmers' cooperative sent their wives and sons to help us too as we surely needed them. We appreciated the people who came, and all the good friends who came to visit.

These people who were strangers to us are here willing to help us. People know who your friends really are when you suffer the loss of a loved one. A good man brought a nice pine box and the woman named Lalaurie brought a new suit of clothes that she sells as a seamstress. Delephine cleaned up Mister Jeremy. She shaved his face, dressed him well, and combed his hair. She asked me to pick him up and put him in the coffin. She could not bring herself to do so. I felt like I had swallowed a stone as I helped her get things ready. Friends came to help us do our many chores. Later we asked some men to bring the coffin to outside the house as it was now too crowded to have a proper wake in the front room of the house. People gathered around to show respect and say "good bye" to a friend. Father would be proud to see so many people here. They gather together to bid him a good journey.

The constable later came from Pineville. He asked us what we thought was the cause of death? We said it looked like the Typhoid. He agreed and he wrote out the death certificate. We thanked him. We put the certificate in the Bible for safe keeping. It grew dark and the oil lanterns are all lit. A small smudge fire is made outside to scare off the mosquitoes. Some lit torches and placed them well. I asked to speak first, and then the many friends gathered here get to say their peace until all can pay their proper respects. We have planned a grand wake for our father: Mister Jeremy Aaron Mack Guffey. His wish is that at the end of his wake that we drink a toast to him with the muscadine grape wine that he is fond of. A few popular hymns are sung. People talked in small groups, mostly in whispers. Some spoke boldly with great stories of him as a younger man being a fine sailor! He never spoke of such things before, so this was news to us. It just shows that you can never know everything about someone, even if you have known them every day for over twenty years!

We went about and tried to thank the people that came here. There are many of his friends that I did not know so well. Several men called him "Mack" in a way that sounded like they have a high regard for him as a good friend. I am sad but I am trying to be friendly to all that came. I was so sad but I have to wait to really mourn as I should. It is almost like a bad dream that he is gone. We are strong for the sake of our father and all that he has done for us. I am afraid so I pray for wisdom to do what is right. My hope is that he would be proud of us doing as he has taught us. We all got up and spoke about our good friendship together. I wished him peace in the next life. I spoke well as I have figured out what best to say beforehand. He would be proud to see so many good friends who have come to pay their respects. A single person's life touches so many people. We then passed out many gourds cut in half for use as simple cups. We opened up the old wine bottles and drank a toast in his honor. Then the feast that the people brought was over whelming! We all talked, and visited until the candles burned low. Some men dug a grave for him. We asked them to wait to bury him until the morning came as he wished. We moved the pine box back into the front room for the night. People brought sunflowers and wild roses to place them over his coffin. It was most thoughtful and lovely to see.

The crowd of people was great last night. More people have come since sundown. People told such great stories and they sang many songs as a tribute. People clapped and sang in a way that was joyful. It made my heart glad as father would enjoy such things. Some people camped around here and to the next hills because it was so late. We tried to keep our eyes open to keep watch on things. Our cattle, horses, and goods are in peril with so many odd folks and strangers about. Worrying about everything is foolish because we are blessed more than most. Most are just people from different places with odd ways of doing things, to us. We are responsible to keep this land trusted to us in good order as we promised our father. Today we have a quiet burial like Mister Jeremy wanted. It all seemed like a bad dream. Some people stayed over and they sang hymns. A man played the fiddle and a woman played the dulcimer. A young man played on a small drum. The wonderful song called "the Amazing Grace" was sung softly as we put the dirt over our father and friend. We both cried and we sang along the best we could. I tried to sing but my throat was hoarse from talking too much. I could not think of anything but the loss of my father. Delephine was right beside me. She was brave for both our sake's.

I looked up and saw a golden eagle fly overhead. I saw this wonderful bird. It made my heart glad as father loved to watch them as we worked in the fields. It flew towards the sun until it was no longer visible. Our father is at peace so we have much to do. No one will take his place. I have some big shoes to try to fill. Friends from the farmer's co-operative will take our wheat to the grist mill and see that things are done for us for a week. It was nice to have that burden off us, but we had so looked forward to our trip to Shreveport together.

November and December 1834. Months have passed and we have lived the best that we can. Christmas came and went but we have no joy in our lives since our father was gone. A new year arrived. The winter cold froze the river solid. We just stayed warm the best we could and ate from the smokehouse. We lost two cows from the terrible cold so I used an axe to butcher them for food. It was too cold to hunt so it was a good thing after all. Had it been in the summer heat, then those cows would have gone to waste since we could not butcher them quick enough before they spoiled. So we thank the good Lord for all His blessings. It may not make sense to us at the time but somehow things work out for the best. I was sick for over two weeks so Delephine healed me up with her bag of good cures. She stayed well so that was good for us both.

January 1835. The Widow Lalaurie came by to sell us some handsome coats and quilts she made. She grew tired so we asked her to stay as the weather turned cold again after two days of fair weather. A big sleet storm came that lasted almost a week. She stayed with us well over a month because she was doing so poorly. Being alone must be hard on a body. We did not mind as it is always nice to be in touch with our elders: as they know so much wisdom and they have many answers that I don't begin to know. Widow Lalaurie looked through our medicine bag to give us some hints on what plants we need to get to keep the medicine bag stocked with cures for when spring and fall comes. She made it nicer here with all her good help by cooking so well. Mending all our clothes to make us look nice for when we travel to trade days. Delephine's biscuits now no longer look like mud bricks! Her cooking has become a delight for all the senses. We put a dry roof over the widow's head and that was the least we could do for such a wonderful woman. She looked better today than she has in weeks. This feels like more of a home. It was nice to have her company. She made the best coffee and she was such a happy, sweet soul. She liked to read the Bible. We had long talks about that and what her early life was like on the

Bayou Pierre. She was a member of the Chitimacha tribe. She married a Frenchman that traded hides. She said that she has a daughter Azalee that moved far away to a northern state. Her son Moses lives in Pineville but she has not seen him in years. It seems odd that someone so nice has lost touch with her children, or that they have abandoned her as it seems. She has kind words for them just the same. We will be her family if no one else will as she is a precious woman.

February 2, 1835. We have a good day of weather so we went out to get some firewood. Our smoke house is about empty so I need to hunt something good to eat. She went with us to make some rabbit snares. She knew a great deal about tracking the different animals because she found a good spot that was promising. She had me bend back some young trees and tie them back with some rope. She put some vegetables in the place where the trap would be sprung. We went back in the brush and tried to be quiet so our dinner time would hurry up. She showed us some medicine plants while we waited. She took up some cattails to show us that the root was good to eat. She rubbed the dirt away as she started eating them. She offered us some and it wasn't too bad since it tasted like a cucumber, and a bit like a red onion. We soon had some plump rabbits caught in a few hours. She also pulled up some reeds and vines to make baskets. We crossed path with an old Chitimacha woman who recognized her.

They cry like all Caddo people do when they meet someone. Soon they talked up a storm as she is a relation of some sort. She cried and laughed a great deal as they visited for the longest time. The woman hugged us because she is one of the pottery and basket-makers that Delephine knows from trade day. They dressed out the rabbits while we made a good fire. We cooked them up good so it made for a nice day together by having a visit with one of her family. We gave her the rabbit pelts. I learned something new about hunting and about medicine plants. The Widow is good to us like she is our very own mother. I also found out that the Bayou Pierre is still a place for families to grow and prosper. One day we will have our own family if we are so fortunate.

February 21. We went in this morning to wake Widow Lalaurie. She has passed away! It made us sad because it reminded us about losing our father all over again. Still she did not die alone so that was some small consolation to us. She died happy with people that cared about her. We have a decent time to travel the next days so we took her in the wagon to Pineville where her son lived so he could give her a decent burial. Delephine dressed her in a nice dress and we put her in a shroud made from one of her quilt tops she made. We passed by her house to get some of her belongings to give her son. Her roof has fallen in so her home was like living outdoors in the middle of the terrible winter! She came to us for refuge, so we were glad things happened like they did. We no longer felt bad as we understand it all better. People do not want pity as they just want to feel useful and to belong somewhere. We arrived at Pineville but her son Moses was not pleased to see us at all. He did not want to appreciate our help because he seemed to be such a selfish person. He thought that we wanted something from him, but we just said our peace so she would have a decent burial. He did not care or seem interested in helping his own mother, so we will bring her back home for a proper burial. We left for home before the weather turned bad or our temper flared up again. I did not know how such a nice woman could have such a skunk for a son! I try not to judge people but he was most hateful to us. It was hard to believe that he was related to such a sweet woman. Delephine said not to bring her back to the Chitimacha tribe because they do not like to deal with death, or a dead body. They will travel a mile around a deceased person from a story she was told. So that was that. We brought her back home. We buried her next to Mister Jeremy so it seemed proper to let her rest here since she was welcome in our home on her last days. We have a quiet burial as it was just for us to attend to this. I said some good prayers and read her favorite scriptures over her. We felt better knowing that she was given a decent resting place with the proper respect for an elder who treated us well as her own family. It started to thunder and rain hard so we hurried inside. Tears went down our faces for the loss of our sweet friend.

The next day was abruptly colder so we bundled up in the quilts that Widow Lalaurie made. This was a big comfort that she would have enjoyed. Delephine made some of her good coffee. She is using her recipe to make some baked goods to go along with it. We wrote her name in our Bible, but we did not know her first name because she is our elder. We could not call her by that name. We will tell the proper authorities when spring comes. The cold continues to keep us indoors, so we try to read and write better. We wrote out a good letter to the constable in Pineville to send him when the better weather comes. We will miss our sweet friend. She treated us well, like she was our own mother. She has earned her reward to be with the Lord.

March 2, 1835. Spring came and the river thawed out good. It flooded the fields for over a week. Then it finally dried out enough to where we did not sink up to our knees in the mud. The floods did bring some nice mud to make the rich dirt for us to plow soon. We got some nice chickens to add to our yard birds. A young peddler came. He had a full wagon loaded with a big pen in the back. We traded him some beef flanks from the smokehouse. He was most happy with the barter we made. We had no money but it seems that barter is best these days. He was heading for Pineville in a few days so we sent our letter with him for the constable to know of Widow Lalaurie passing. We have some nice chickens since ours were thinned out by the cold, hungry raccoons, and that awful chicken snake we killed. Delephine likes the good eggs and now she can enjoy something decent to cook now and then. The yard birds thin out the bugs and we get the good eggs to trade from what we don't need. It raised our spirits to have some new animals and a visitor to talk with about recent news. The Cherokee have now settled in piney woods of east Texas. They have made quite a good trade at Shreveport for salt, hides, and horses. We hope soon to go to Shreveport sometimes for a few days. We always want to get some time to get out and see what is beyond the Cane River.

March 4, 1835. We picked some new land to break. It is a bit stony so we will take a day or two to clear it of all the rocks. We hitched the wagon to move the stones out. We got the bed of the wagon loaded down with stones. By four in the afternoon it is clouding up by threatening to rain. We headed for the barn, and got the horses fed and watered. The rain just came down in sheets, followed by much lightning. We slept on and off. We went down to the root cellar to wait out the bad storm. Just when the rain was going to let up a new wave of storms came. We finally get to sleep and hope for a better day tomorrow. Our days are too full not to get more work than this done!

March 5, 1835. Today we have a bigger flood. A "gully washer": a real "frog floater"! The tin can that we use for a rain gauge has long overflowed. That means that it rained over five inches since yesterday! After two months of drought, we get some good relief. All in one full day's time. Our juju trees on the hill survived the flood. We will have plentiful crops of wheat this growing season. Next season will plant okra and its cousin, cotton. They were brought from the distant Africa like our people were. This is now our home, for we would be strangers there to what would be our own people. We will make our own way in the world as this is where we really belong. Life is hard without our father being here to help guide us. What would he think of us these days? Would he be proud of us or would he be angry at us? We also miss the sweet Widow Lalaurie. Life is hard living here. I always wonder what to do next. How can Delephine stand to live here with me? As all I can do is never quite enough.

March 8. Delephine and I are making plans for spring. This gives us hope for the future. The many days of cold without seeing the sun, just left us in a funk. Things are starting to green up as the leaves are all coming out. The sun is visible. It is warmer and it feels so good on my face. We are getting past the troubles we have been feeling in these past months. We would like to make this farm our own home. A man came to pay us for our last wheat crop that the co-operative made for us when father passed. He visited and talked about everything he knew. He paid in in silver, which was something we haven't seen in a long while. We don't get out much to have many visitors, so it was nice to have some company. The rumor from the flourmill is that General Mexia is like Santa Anna's own right arm. He is in this area looking for cattle and horses to outfit his army. He has talked to a few people headed back from Texas. They said that General Mexia might come this far north to make raids after crossing the Sabine River. We won't be caught unaware if this Mexia is bold to cross the Sabine. We will keep watch for any loss from rustling or anyone who wishes to do us harm. We are strong and will continue on as we should. We work too hard to have our things taken away as some have lost much of their stock, security, and peace of mind.

March 10, 1835. We have no more word of Mexican General Mexia. If his troops are about they haven't shown themselves. We have lost much sleep staying up watching for trouble. Our trouble will be that we need a full night to sleep. That has been in short supply for a while. We have been short tempered with each other because we are tired. Living out here without our father's help has been difficult. We pray for wisdom and patience to know what to do best. I took out a piece of paper to draw out a plot of our property by the river. We planned out what would grow best so that we would better use the fields to make our yield better. Delephine said for us to grow some potatoes. It would be good to have a crop of new potatoes for a change.

March 12. We set about to finish clearing the land that is newly broken. We start planting the new land with some onions and peppers that grow so well here. Wheat is to be the best crop this year as prices are higher at the trading post for flour. We plant different crops from year to year to help make our land prosper. We keep stock of what grows best. The floods gave us much good dirt from down river that is so red and full of iron. We traded a cow for some seed and a decent plow. The seed pots are full so there is much to put to good use. The older peddler is a preacher who came through to sell red onion sets and potato slips to support himself. I ran a harrow over the field and the preacher walked besides me to preach as I worked. He scared the horse some because he talked so loud. He stayed for a day and he even planted a field with us to help out. We fed him good so he would be back through as he could return on the loop to New Orleans. Delephine boiled him some eggs and made a pan of cornbread to take with him. He would be back as his trade as a traveling preacher took him far and wide. Company is always welcome as we get to hear more about the outside world so we focus less on our own problems.

March 14. We found some red clay to make jars, bowls, and clay baskets. Barter at trade day came for some decent cloth and leather for a new harness. The local women get together with some elder Chitimacha women who sell cane baskets, bowls and pots besides the road. They take great pride in making clay goods so we let them get in and dig all the good clay that they want. They always "cry" when they greet people because they are glad to see you. They hug you like you are their own children! They give us corn cakes and they like to play with our hair. It is their way of doing things, so we always welcome them as friends as they have always been peaceful neighbors to us for many years. Delephine knows many of their words so she can talk with them. They also do sign-talking which I mostly knew the greetings and trade signs. Tonight they have dug out a fire pit to put charcoals and hard wood in to cure out the goods that they have dried well enough to bake them out. They mixed sand with the clay to be up to holding water and rough use. They all talk and carry on so much as they roll the coils for the baskets. It is scraped smooth with a piece of gourd. They do not eat for a few days as they work all day and most of the night. I brought them food and they ran me off as it brings bad luck in their traditions to be disturbed by a man during the baking of the pots. I heard the sounds of a panther about so I built a big fire to keep it away. I wasn't so terrible then because they were sorely afraid of the big cat being about.

The women stay over a week so they have too many pots to carry. They took sumac plants to boil in a tin pot to make black and brown colors. They had me collect dandelions to make purple, and goldenrod flowers to make yellow paint to decorate the pots with. I told Delephine to tell them that I would take them back to their village when they get ready to go. They are in no hurry to leave until they are happy with all they have made. They are more than just some clay pots: they are making something special and wonderful to store food and water in. Each pot almost had a life of its own because of the animals and how the women made them so special. I marveled over their work. They allowed me to look them over and I put my favorite ones to one side. I had to say why I did not like the others. I liked the fish and turtle pots because they reminded of my days fishing on the Cane River. The ones that looked like people were not anyone I knew. They were scary because these looked odd like some kind of a ghost. Delephine told them what I said, so they were happy then and I was back in their good graces. It grew too dark for them to travel so far with a panther about. That was one of the many pots they made in honor of that beast. I offered to take them back in the morning when it was first light.

March 20. We hitch up the wagon to take them to their village. The wagon is full of big clay pots. Delephine said they cook in them by throwing in hot lumps of clay scooped from a fire. Water jugs and storage pots came next as the majority are shaped like animals. They made pots shaped like bears, turtles, fish, armadillos, alligators, pelicans, herons, panthers, and water snakes. They are all most curious because they reflect their own hunting stories and beliefs. Delephine told me the many curious things that they say. The Caddo refuse to ride in the wagon because they are afraid of the wagon wheels that turn! Delephine also walks behind it to make more room for all the pots to ride well. We arrive to their summer camp. They all begin the "crying greeting" which starts until the majority of them to see that we are friendly or not. This is a ploy because all their warriors have circled around me to see if I am their enemy. They don't seem to like the wagon either, so I hold up a new pot and make the "trade" signs. The elder women catch up to the wagon. They run to scold the warriors who come too close. "Tey-sha!" is their words to the warriors. They are telling them we are good friends. Most are sweet people who could be fierce if you were on their bad side. I would never try to find out what that might be. They put down their long, feathered darts and sharp pointed weapons that could be thrown at us. They do not use the bow, but still they are great hunters by all the pelts that are stacked up for trade. Their elder women are called "Qualls" who do all the talking. The men just listen as they have little chance to argue back very much! It looks like it would do little good to try! Even their chief is trying to appease one woman who was not getting enough help with her lodge building notions. Some of their men are warriors, and some are set to be farmers depending on what the Qualls want them to do. I am staying on their good side so they won't put me to work too! It is enough to keep up with Delephine. She laughs at me because she knows I am trying to stay out of the path of trouble. She offers to set them against me if I don't do right. She knows she has me where she wants me, so I am agreeable as who can argue with a woman? Where does it get you if you do? Not too far.

We all unloaded the clay pots so they hold them up to have a good dance because this is the day called "Winter Count" where they celebrate surviving the terrible winter. Delephine dances and they pull me out to dance too. They laugh and they are a sweet people. They then pass around all the babies born during the winter to introduce them to the tribe. They give them the names they are to be known by. We will now be their friends so we will not feel uncomfortable if we cross paths in the future. They gave us some bone and bead necklaces to wear that show we are welcome. These allow us to attend their trade days and celebrations as the seasons change. Out here on the Bayou Pierre it is better to make friends than chance death by having an enemy.

March 22, 1835. We have lost two of our best milk cows and four horses. We said that it may have been men of Generals Mexia and Cos. We are thinking that it may be someone just is plain stealing! The Sabine trade has brought many more people here with their own notions of how to get something for nothing! They may have watched us out in the fields as we were busy working late yesterday. We have been watching for them today. They are figuring that after plowing all day that we would not hear them stealing. We followed their tracks as they split off in different directions, unto hard and rocky ground. We lost their trail as it is too close to established hideouts. I cut across the trail to take a short cut through the Kisatchie forest past the tall hills. There was a camp of many rough looking men. I hid my horse and broke off a big limb and held it in front of me like I saw a Chitimacha hunter do one day. I put wet clay-dirt on my face so I could hide in plain sight. I later watched another large group of men ride by with our horses and cattle. They also have numerous cattle and horses that have several brands that I recognized. Among them all was that Mister Harris, the local constable and a few people from the funeral! They are playing both sides of the fence by working against us and the law. I grew very angry and almost stopped breathing for a bit. Then I sweated a great deal as tears came to my eyes. I already knew that it would be at too great a disadvantage to get them back. So I came home knowing it is better to be alive with a loss of our cattle than to face a terrible death. It was just at too much of a risk to get them back. Then where would Delephine be? Riding home with the thought of just being safe on my own land is all that mattered at this point. I put up old Radish in the barn. This tired mare is all that we have left of any value. The wife has a big feast to celebrate my safe return. She is a glorious sight! She is good as any gold! Even when she scolds me, she is a wonder to me. She does that so often: for good reason, I figure. Someone has to keep me in line now that Mister Jeremy is gone. A good woman does much to get things done around here. I would be lost without her and her without me.

Delephine was dressed nice in an outfit that she made for the trip to Shreveport. She welcomed me home like I was a king. She cried and fussed at me for making her worry. We talked and just celebrated being together. That was all that is important: more than any number of cows, or anything else. The thing that scared me most was that she would be mad or disappointed in me. That wasn't the case at all! We are happy to just live a simple life. Still it is hard to lose something we worked so hard to raise. Father would understand if he were here. He raised us to use some common sense. We will pick and choose our battles so we can live to fight another day. We forgive them as the Lord forgave us. Still it is not easy as it takes away what little we have.

March 24. We have lost more of our stock during the night, right under our nose. All the smuggling going back and forth

has always been so much trouble. We have always tried to stay clear of it all. It seems that we will be a regular target every time they pass by. We will keep ourselves clear of trouble, but trouble is looking at us from all the losses of property that we have. I feel that we can stay here another year, and start over in Texas. Texas might be better once the Mexican army settles all their issues with the new white settlers. The Mexicans wish them to speak only Spanish and become a Catholic, I heard at the gristmill. They fear that if the language changes from Spanish to English or that another religion comes there then they will lose their control of the settlers there in south Texas. They may have lost Texas already. All rumors carry some bit of truth. Some parts of rumor are hard to field as what is the truth? The truth is what you make of it. Good or bad, that is how it is.

March 25. We set out to get some plowing done. We finally bought a fair plow horse for twenty dollars from the man at the gristmill. We had no choice but to pay more for it since the price of horses and cattle have went up with so much stealing going on. Today a light wind keeps the work from being so hard. We drew out a plan on the paper to get a rough idea of how it would all go. It was suited to grow wheat this year the farmer's almanac states. We studied which phase of the moon was best to plant on. We got out our best sorrow to put unto the plow. The ground is very sandy here, so it was a fair amount of effort for Sadie, our "little mule" as we call her. She works like one, even if she does not look like one. She keeps being good help to me in my chores around here. Delephine calls me "Big Mule". The new ground is tough going. We have burned it to clear it off. I used a good harrow to break it for new planting. We plow 4 more acres this week. We later worked on a better map of the farm land to allow for the drainage of water, and plot the trees on the land are good landmarks. We marked it all down so we could better plan out the new fields.

March 27. We have seen signs of many strangers camping nearby. That does not make them the thieves that we are seeking. We keep a healthy distance from them. They will pass us by soon enough. Tonight, we will drink strong coffee to keep a better watch over our place. We pray a lot, also. We keep our eyes open until dawn and nothing ever happened. We go to sleep for a few hours to find ourselves woke up by smoke, and the baying of our old mare. Our hay barn is set a fire! I manager to get her out before it all falls in. I tripped in the dark and got up to find something out of place: there is also a warning painted on a cotton seed sack set on our porch. It was heavy like it was full of rocks. I started to toss it away until I heard the clink of silver coins inside. It is a sound I would not forget as I have only heard it at trade day among the big vendors.

The warning said that we should take this sack of silver dollars. We are to go away from this farm by the end of the week! They will burn the house and us with it! Burning our barn was just a warning of what will come next if we stay! We talked about our choices. We did not like our choices as we have just one. One choice is better than none. We will have to go from here to leave all our hard work behind us. The choice is clear: that one man alone has no chance to protect himself, or his property. We will have to gather together all our valuables. Delephine gets the big trunk and she puts what little we have that is ours. She is angry and scared so she does not talk to me. I prayed over what to do as there seems to be no good answers for her to stop crying.

March 28. I surveyed the area to see if there were any tools I could save from the barn's ashes. It finally cooled off enough to go through. Inside I found a saw blade, a grubbing hoe and several axe heads. All what was left of a good sledge hammer was the head with half a handle. Little was left of any use to us.

Then I found a skeleton of what looked like a man that was trapped in the burning barn! Things went from bad to worse. His hands looked to be tied behind him! The same was true of his ankles as there was a chain around them. He had a knife sticking in his right side. I felt sick as I did not know how to tell Delephine about this one. I got very ill so I went down to the well to wash my face. Then I went to tell her. I hugged her and she pulled me back to figure out what was going on. She patiently waited for me to speak my mind as she has a few things to say. She found another note tacked to our wagon bed with a knife. It was telling us to leave by the end of this week or that we will die! There are 50 more silver dollars in another cottonseed sack! These people must be crazy! Smugglers must want our place very bad to bribe us to leave with money and threats! That skeleton was left to show us what might happen to us if we stay here! I showed Delephine what I found in the ashes of the barn. She cried a great deal for the longest time. I held her to be brave for both our sakes. She cried until she shook and I cried too because I was so mad. This bayou has become a place of death with nothing happy left here. It was a tough place to be. It makes it hard to stay here, to make any new plans.

We took some time to sit down to eat as a full day has passed without a single bite of food. We ate some beef jerky as we counted out a total of 250 silver dollars! We have never seen that much silver in one place in a long time. It will take that to start over in Texas, as soon as we can get all packed and ready. We feel that some smugglers want our farm to serve as a hideout, since they are so desperate for us to go. They paid us for our trouble, so we will go in the morning.

That is that! We will leave for Texas for the people at the Pineville gristmill always want to go there. We will start all over and build a new home as we have in Flatwoods. It is sad to leave here. I pray over what to do here as I buried the bones I found in the barn's ashes. I placed them in a blanket and wrapped them in a respectful way to show them a proper burial.

We pay our last respects to Mister. Jeremy's grave. Delephine planted some flower seeds around Widow Lalaurie's grave as I covered the graves with some river stones to make them well marked. I made a cross for the new grave with two axe handles I found partly burned in the ashes. I used the chain wrapped around its ankles to hold the cross together. That seemed proper. We rested for a few hours to try to gather up our sense of what to do next. I grew ill again so I went to the well to pour a bucket of water over my head. Delephine gets ready to finish some packing and taking stock of our goods. Mister Jeremy would have us leave this place rather than to perish here. We might have to stop at Shreveport to stock up at the trading post before we cross over into Texas. I think about the years that we have lived here, and all the work we have done. This land has earned our sweat and blood. Alone we are nothing if we die trying to stay here. Who will bury us, or who would care for this place like we do? We have few choices. None of them are very easy to do.

Tonight I read ISAIAH, Chapter 28, verses 23-29, "The Plowman."

We quickly divided the silver dollars into fifty per coffee sack. We put one in the water barrel. Then Delephine put the rest them in the wood box of the wagon. Then I nailed it down good. We did notice that our wagon ruts are a bit deeper than most since we are loaded down good. Hopefully we will be in a secure spot soon. We will have to rest our horses more often. They will have a lot of buffalo grass to eat, and be strong. We have not covered as much ground as we would have liked, but we have to be practical. We must not over burden ourselves, or the horses. I took the lantern from the front porch, lit it and dashed it against the front of the house. Now the house will match the old barn! If some bold gunrunners or smugglers want to take our house then they can build their own hideout for their own use! Delephine fussed at me but it was too late. She said that I was always looking over the next hill, so here was my chance to leave here for good! I understood about her being angry but I have too many other things to think about. I wondered about the skeleton we found in the ashes of the barn. He was left there on purpose. Was his family still looking for him?

It all seemed crazy. Leaving off to a strange place is not my first choice of what to do. Dying is not my choice either, so it is the lesser of two evils. This Eden has its share of snakes. We are being pushed out of the garden, for a good cause. It means saving our dear lives. There is no coming back since we are no longer welcome here.

Chapter Two

The Trading Post at Shreveport.

March 31, 1835. We traveled all day until the sun went down. Delephine cried more with every mile that passed. She is leaving the only home she knows. I stopped and rested our horse as she is old and she can't go much farther. We are at the last watering hole before the trading post. We might get there by midnight if we leave soon. Delephine was tired from the road. She can stack wheat all day, but not do so well riding too long in a wagon on a long bumpy road. We made a fire and cooked the two rabbits we shot. A man passed with several horses tethered on a long reign in a remuda. The man had not eaten for over a day so we offered him one of our cooked rabbits. He was so happy to get to eat and rest from the road. He reminded us of our wonderful father. We gave him a blanket. He offered us a two of his four horses for sale.

We talked and struck a deal as he was more agreeable with a full belly. We wrote out a bill of sale and he signed it with his mark since he could not write. Now we have decent horses for a team as old Radish has come up lame. The man offered to take her off our hands as she would be meat for his table. It made me sad, but we could not leave her out here for the wolves. I gave the man five silver dollars. He just about fell over when he saw we had them. He rubbed it across his face like he was dreaming. He cut the coin with a knife to see that it was real silver. Money has been so tight this past year that all we could was barter for goods, until a few days ago. I hope that it was not a mistake to buy these horses with silver, but we have no choice but to have a way to pull the wagon to Shreveport by tomorrow. We woke early and made coffee and gave some to the man. We did not talk much. He gave us the blanket back but we told him that he can keep it. We parted company on good terms. The new horses made our old wagon look shabby. It was like wearing a new shirt with an old pair of pants. We might find a newer wagon at the trading post. I talked to Delephine about it. She agreed with me, for once. Leaving home and all that we know makes us both uncertain. I can't afford to show any weakness for it brings up more of her fears for the future. Our faith holds us tight and brings us back to reason. It is all we have and all we know to do.

April 1, 1835. We arrive at Shreveport and travel to the
trading post. There are many saloons and several vendors
selling food along the road. We did stop to eat as the food
smelled so good. We had some beef stew, corn bread, and
hot coffee. The new horses found some lush grass and a nice
watering hole. A man stopped us and asked for fifty cents to
let the horses eat the grass and drink at "his" pond. I have
never heard of such a thing on a public road. I did not want
to start any trouble being a stranger in this town. We later
saw the place we would usually go for the trade day. The
grass has now grown back from being burned off. I thought
about our earlier plans to come here. It was much different
than I remembered. We finally made it to the trading post by
sundown. I have Delephine get the shopping lists we made
handy. We took out one little sack of silver dollars to buy
goods. I figured about sixty dollars is plenty to buy all the
goods and tools that we need. Once we cross over the Sabine
into Texas we may not have as many choices, or have to pay
twice what it costs here. I stuck the bag of coins under my
belt for safekeeping. Delephine stayed in the wagon to keep
an eye on what little we own and keep our new horses safe.
She is to shoot off the old pistol if she has any trouble to call
me outside for some help. We can hurry up and get this over
with so we can get on our way to Texas. Texas sounds better
by the day, so we hurry to go.

I went inside the trading post to find a bunch of jaspers playing cards and drinking strong drink. The smoke rolls outside when I opened the front door. The windows are nailed shut to keep out trouble. It may be to keep trouble bottled up! Two oil lamps were burning bright but it was dark in places of the cluttered room because the room was so smoky. They all stopped their card games as they looked harshly at me like I was a horse at an auction. They had some unkind words for me interrupting their fun. I ignored them and asked for the owner. He threw down his cards as he got up and settled his debts. He then walked over to see what I wanted. I got out my list and he looked it up and down. He said that he could not give credit to a dirt farmer like me! I was not asking for any charity and I told him so! The men kept playing cards and they kept watching me to see if I was going to fight with him. I acted calm to ask if he had any of those wagons outside for sale. He does and he offered a good deal on a new one with an extra wagon wheel. This was no time to cut corners on buying a cheap wagon that won't last for long. He said that he has a good wagoner and some good carpenters for hire to build stout cabins. I agree to buy the wagon and the many goods on my list. He seemed to wonder how I was going to pay for everything. I pointed at my money pouch tied to my belt. He shook his head in disbelief thinking I was making a joke.

We heard two gunshots so several of us ran outside. Delephine has just shot a snake that was hanging down from a tree above the wagon. One of the men picked it up to see what it was. "It is a 'shoulder draper': a poisonous water snake that lives in the trees after a heavy rain. She hit it twice. Once in the head and then she shot it almost in half!" The men marveled over her fine aim. They took off their hats to show their proper respect to her. A few cards fell out of one of the men's hats. They had words with each other and pushed each other about like some small boys do. Delephine handed me another sack of coins. She looked serious and she had a few words to say. "I don't like snakes or coyotes! Maybe you-all could hurry up because we have to get to Texas by tomorrow!" She reloaded the gun and rolled the gun against her right thigh to show it off. She stuck it back into her belt to secure it. The men took stock of her words. I had to hold my peace as I was tickled at my woman's attitude towards the strangers. She wasn't "play acting" as she was just tired and ready to get going. We hurried back inside to finish our shopping. The men joked, "I know who wears the pants in your household!" I smiled and said, "I know who wears the gun! That is all that matters." The men laughed and patted me on the back. They liked that my woman was so stout and contrary. A good woman has to be tough as any man to survive out here.

We took stock of all the goods we have. He even threw in some nice cotton cloth and a blue dress for my woman. He also had a nice bonnet he added to make her happy. He wanted to stay on her good side, as I do all so often. He said that the wagon with the old one for trade and the goods in all were about seventy five dollars. He added a new water barrel, a good map, a flint and steel striker, three knives, half a keg of iron nails and a pound of salt. We shook hands on the deal. The owner joked to me, "Santa 'Annie' had better look out for when your wife crosses the Sabine! Those Indians too! If I had a dollar for everyone that bragged about finding new riches as they crossed over into Texas, then I would own half of Shreveport!" They bad mouthed Texas as a bad place to live. I smiled politely and pulled out the cash sacks. The men grew quiet as I counted out the silver dollars. I sweated as I stacked them ten coins tall in seven rows. Then I counted out five more and put the rest back. Their eyes were big as the full moon. It was like a hungry dog watching you eat your dinner. One of the men asked if I was a gunrunner. I said that I am just a dirt farmer! They laughed and thought I was joking. "Farmers come here and don't have two nickels to rub together, always wanting something on credit!" I just went on and gave it no more thought as we are strangers and I did not have to account to anyone here. They ain't anybody to be pointing some fingers!

One of the men helped load up the wagon. Delephine was drinking from the well as she stretched her legs and tired back. She then aimed the pistol at different places like she had a mind to find a new target. The man hurried to help load the wagon much faster. I held back laughing as she was putting on a front to make them act respectable towards us. It worked and we got loaded up in good time. The men inside were looking out through the dirty windows. Our visit gave them something good to wonder about. We are no thieves or gunrunners. We are just here as some dirt farmers with a better chance to start over: brand new.

I drove along and then stopped a mile out and fretted over the fact that I did not move the other money bags from their hiding place on the old wagon. Delephine has taken care of all that when I went back inside to settle up. She had my back covered and I was bewildered trying to keep up with all that I needed to remember to do. What a relief it was to me to get out of there in one piece. Shreveport might be our last view of "civilization" for a while. It wasn't very civilized as I could see. Texas could only be better than this!

We crossed over the Sabine River on the raft crossing. The river ran not too deep but swift enough to be trouble with a loaded-down wagon. We paid fifty cents to the ferryman and Delephine was mad because of all the money we have spent since we left the Bayou Pierre. I assured her that we should go easy on the horses with a new wagon. Being on a deep river that has so many sandbars and drop-offs was most troublesome. It was fifty cents well spent. She gave me a dollar's worth of worry, over nothing! She was mad at me for a while. It was a long ride across the prairie called the Elysian Fields towards the main Texas trail. I saw Trammel's Trace marked fairly well, but it was a longer route to get there. The other roads still had bad ruts from the last rain so it was a wonder to figure out which way to go. I found a good spot to camp among the cedars. Delephine did not like this. She saw the fire and smoke from a distant campfire. It was not from anyone that we knew of. She felt it was someone from the trading post tracking us. We rested the horses and left out without sleeping. The open prairies soon became hills and pine trees. My head hurt and she took pity on me. She picked a good spot so I pulled down some tree limbs and water sprouts to hide our wagon better. We did not have a campfire or coffee. We ate some beef jerky. We took turns keeping good a watch. Each of us can rest but our backs hurt from riding so long in the wagon, and from sleeping on the ground a few days.

April 2, 1835. There are notices nailed to the trees along the trail, telling of homesteading in Texas. Every adult male can claim 4,600 acres if married. 1,534 acres if a single man settles here. Women can band together to get a single land grant. The Texans want settlers to come and hold the land to help with their cause: to protect Texas from more Mexican raids. We will homestead some land, and raise our family here. The banner on the tree says that we should go to Nacogdoches to talk with General Sam Houston, the head of the Texas army and a lawyer interested in the growth of the settlements. We are wondering if freedmen are allowed to own land here, and if anyone will respect our claim to the land? Last time we had a choice to leave Louisiana, but now we may not be so fortunate to have another good chance again.

We travel down to the outskirts of Nacogdoches.

April 4, 1835. We come into town on the main road. It has been a very dusty road. The town square is large with many stores and nice buildings. It is not as busy with wagons and strangers as Jefferson or Shreveport. We found the lawyer's office marked on the east side of the square. We tied our wagon secure, and paid a boy a nickel to water our team of horses. Inside the livery stable talking to each other to see who is the livery manager. In rides a tall man on a big white horse. We asked the tall man if he is the livery manager. The man smiles and he says, "The manager of this livery is a young boy. It seems that he has gone out fishing somewhere. I am

Sam Houston. But you can call me 'General Sam'. This is the name that many call me by." I told him that we are here to get a land grant. He smiles and looks glad to see us. "Great! Come to my office around ten in the morning. Go down the road to Goyen's hotel. The manager is named Deborah. Tell her that I have recommended you." We both shook his hand and we took his horse and put out some hay to help him out. Delephine brought him a ladle of cool water.

In walks a young boy with a big string of fish across his shoulder. He puts the fish in the horse trough and then he takes care of the horses and secures our wagon. The boy looked surprised to see so many people waiting.

Mister Houston scolded the boy for leaving his job, but Delephine hugged him to praise him for being such a good fisherman. "He is just a boy, not someone in your army! He should be out having some fun. He will have to work like a man soon enough!" Mister Houston smiles as he took off the boy's hat and rubbed his head messing up his hair. He gave him a dollar for all the fish. He asked the boy to give the stringer of fish to Deborah to cook for our diner. Delephine offers to help her as she can cook some good fish well. Deborah accepts her offer as she is spread thin some days. The boy named Aaron is invited too because he needs some attention as he is an orphan. The boy was so excited that he dropped his silver dollar in the hay. We helped him find it and we gave him some kind words too. He cried because he was afraid he was about to lose his job because he went fishing on such a nice day. I told him that I will go with him the next time we visit here. That boy needs a daddy real bad!

We went down to Mister Goyen's store and hotel like Mister Houston suggested. We met Deborah the store and hotel manager. She treated us well and she found us a nice room for a dollar a day with meals. We liked the room. She brought us some stew and a place to take a bath. I shaved my face and got cleaned up. Delephine cut my hair very short. I felt like a new man. Delephine rested a few hours. Later we walked down the main street. There was much to see and do. We sat in a nice shade to talk like we are town people. People were nice to us so we felt welcome here. We saw Deborah running some errands so we talked with her. "Texas is nice, no matter what people in Shreveport say!" She replied, "Shreveport isn't all that, no matter whom you ask in Texas!" Deborah is a happy sort that looks on the positive side of things. We laughed and we walked to the hotel together. I helped carry some of her goods she had in a big basket. She was a busy person that keeps the hotel and store running strong. I wondered how it was to live in a town around people who come from all over. I could not keep up with her. She does the work of a whole crew!

I looked to see Mister Goyens but he was out trading horses with the Cherokee, the boy at the livery said. He has built half this town and he has made jobs here for a good many folks. We went back to Goyen's store. Deborah has some clothes picked out for both of us. She is so thoughtful and there are some good deals for Texas. I got two shirts, a tie and a suit of clothes. Delephine got a red dress and a hat from France. We were spendthrifts but we have done without so much for most of our lives. Since we are going to court then we are to look nice to get our land grant. Delephine got her hair cut by Deborah and she looked so pretty! She gets to wear some French perfume and it was nice to see her get spoiled for a change. She evened-up the haircut that Delephine gave me to make it look nicer. I got the royal treatment. I have never worn anything new before this day so I felt like a much different person getting so much done for me. If I had known that Texas was so nice I would have made it here sooner! We saw ourselves in the big mirror. It would be hard to believe that we are regular dirt farmers! We are living well so we will enjoy things in this town for a few days.

We have a big feast. General Sam was there along with the livery boy named Aaron. Delephine cooked the fish well like we do in Louisiana! Deborah made bread pudding for the boy to enjoy. We just enjoyed being together with a good meal, nice clothes to wear, and a dry roof over our head. We just talked and got to know each other by eating a good meal. It was nice to visit and see what town people live like. A person could get fat living like this for very long. Deborah played the piano as Delephine cleared away the dishes. We helped her as she cooked in a hot kitchen for all our benefit. I was so stuffed I could not keep my eyes open for long. The next day is to be busy so I drank some stout coffee. I wrote down some questions to ask General Houston while Delephine slept. My feet hurt from the new shoes but it was a nice problem to have. I did not know that life could be like this!

April 5. We meet with the lawyer and soldier: General Sam Houston. His office took up a large room, full of books. His desk has many books and notes in stacks like hay. He looks to be very busy, so we ask the questions we wrote down before we slept last night. We have many questions to ask. This Sam Houston is a very tall man. Even sitting down he looks to be a person of great stature. We asked the questions about the rights of freedmen in Texas. He said that we would have to stay a few days until Circuit Judge Ellis B. Thomas comes to settle a land dispute between William Goyens and his neighbor Gus Burton who is being unreasonable over water rights. After the hearing we will be allowed time to speak to the judge to get a ruling. Mister Houston tells us he is impressed that we both can read and write. He showed me a book called the Iliad that he likes. I found our Bible and read a few verses to him. He knew the words from memory as I read them out loud. He finished out the verses I started. I like that he is so smart. He is a highly respected man in this area from what the people here say. We sit down and write out all our concerns to tell the judge. General Sam asked us many questions and we showed him our freedman's letter and Mister Jeremy's will. I also showed him my own questions and concerns. He liked that I had some good questions to ask so that helped him make his court case stronger. He told us to speak in a good tone, and to look the judge in the eyes when we speak. We made progress for over an hour by talking. Now it is time to seek to rest for the night. It has been a long day. It will be good to be back in our room to rest. We sleep well in a secure room far away from the threats of outlaws and thieves. A few more days and we might be ready again to travel after all this gets settled.

April 6, 1835. Circuit judge Ellis B. Thomas will hold court at two in the afternoon, at the town square. William Goyens is another freedman, just like me. He trades horses with the east Texas Cherokee tribe. He is having some big trouble with his neighbor over water rights. His status as a land owner was also in question because he is a freedman and the other man is a citizen of Mexico. We waited for half an hour and the man going against Mister Goyens did not show up. The man named Gus Burton finally rushed into the trial much too late, dressed in his old work clothes. It upset the judge because the man smelled of whiskey and the horse barn. His hair and beard are uncombed. He is quite dirty. He was in need of being downwind of us all! The man named Gus Burton demanded his water rights so much that he tried to talk over the judge. The judge grew angry so he ordered the bailiff to take Burton outside to give him a bath in the horse trough! "We pity the horses that follow behind him!" the judge remarked as he banged his gavel and the bailiff took him outside against his will. That was his "water rights" for being so disrespectful! We are glad that we had a bath earlier and wore nicer clothes than what we work in. We minded our manners because we are already baptized!

Gus Burton will have to take down his rock dam for his gristmill and pay a fine if he does not do this quickly. Mister Houston smiled and waited for the judge's verdict to be documented. He offered to act as bailiff in the meantime. We offered our best behavior. Our court trial came at a good time because William Goyens won his case to keep his close neighbor from damming up the water to his land. Mister Goyens' case in his favor helps make our case stronger. We have to wait a short time until our case comes up. The paperwork is done and the case gets documented in a big book of records. Sam Houston said that Judge Ellis appreciates a nice appearance in court and good manners. He gave us all the good advice needed to get us a land grant. We got out our family Bible and our freedman's letter from Mister Jeremy. We showed it to Mister Houston. He was pleased to see it, for it was a big help towards our case getting our land grant! All of our proof is right here. It is exciting to see we have a real future. At least we won't have to go swimming in the horse trough! The time comes for our case to be heard.

Mister Houston reads our case, and the judge made notes as he listened. The rights of other people, a freed man and his woman are in question. Mister Houston said our letter from Mister Jeremy is called a "manumission" letter that states we are free people. The judge called us 'libres'. That sounded good! He asked, "Do we owe any debts?" We said, "No sir, none." Judge Thomas then said that since we owe no debts, and we are legally free in Louisiana, then we are declared free in Texas, the province of Mexico." Then no other future claims are binding against us! He bangs the gavel so our case has been heard. We thanked the judge, and he said that he is pleased to rule in favor of someone when there is a clear-cut case. Judge Thomas asked Delephine 'how long we have been married?' Delephine then tells him how Mister Jeremy saved us from the slave traders at Baton Rouge when we were children twenty years ago. Then she states that we have not been married yet. The judge smiles and he tells us that we must be married to legally own a land grant. The judge looks stern and he asks me to do what is proper! I felt so terrible. I took stock of myself and got down on one knee. I asked Delephine to marry me. Delephine says, "He has been my best friend all my life. I was wondering if he was ever going to ask me! He just assumes that I am always there!" I looked down at the ground to muster my will to talk. Mister Houston smiles and he motions for me to rise to my feet. The judge asks me to hold Delephine's right hand as we stand next to each other. We agree to marry. She would have me as a husband, after all. General Sam and William Goyens act as the witnesses along with Deborah and three others that are here. We take our wedding vows. I stuttered terribly a few times. Mister Sam Houston asked us to take a last name for ourselves for legal reasons. I said, "Freeman" or Mister Jeremy's last name: "Mack Guffey." Delephine said, "Mack" to make it simpler to remember and to spell. People called him that, so that is how we best remember and honor our father. I thought, "That way none of his other family can try to come to make any claim against us in the near future." Sam Houston writes our name on a wedding license. Then he signed the permit to settle on our land in east Texas. It was a wonderful sight. I wrote all this down carefully, so that no one can argue over what was said if someone tries to claim against us as freed people, or new Texicans. We later take the permit after it is filed with the good judge and General Sam. Delephine took both licenses to put in our Bible.

We are married. I feel happy and terribly scared at the same time! We sign some legal papers. We are to meet this evening with General Houston to get a map of the area of the land grants. He will tell where to best respect the land boundaries of the Indian tribes. He patted us on the back and he offers some great advice for newcomers. We need some good advice so we listened well. We meet for supper with William Goyens and General Houston. We have talk of the map of the land grants, and we have some questions. Mister Goyens talked about how the new grants would affect the relations with the Red River tribes. We have also been asking and addressing some of the concerns that Sam Houston is interested in settling. We talked for the longest time after supper. He said that these two cases coming up have helped establish the rights of freemen and the soon the rights of Indians that needs to be resolved. Both cases being heard at the same time was a stroke of good fortune in our favor. General Sam is getting ready to leave to go to Washington City, the capitol of the Northern Federal States. His notion is to get their aid in securing help in the form of more men coming to Texas to help settle the state of affairs with Mexico. The land grants are the biggest enticement. We wish him well. He said that the provisional governor Henry Smith is urging the Texicans to be separate from Mexican rule. He feels that the Federal States will be sympathetic to our struggle with Generals Mexia, Santa Anna, and Cos. We wished him well, and gave him our support against any invaders. He said that, "I will need your help, and the help of all our people." We talked a while and had a good talk. Then we parted company, and went our different ways, being on good terms.

Tonight we read Roman Chapter 8 verse 15-17. "For ye have not received the spirit of bondage again to fear; but ye have received the spirit of adoption, whereby we cry, Abba, Father! The Spirit itself beareth witness with our spirit that we are children of God: And if children, then heirs of God, and joint-heirs with Christ Jesus. If so, being that we suffer with Him, that we may be glorified together.

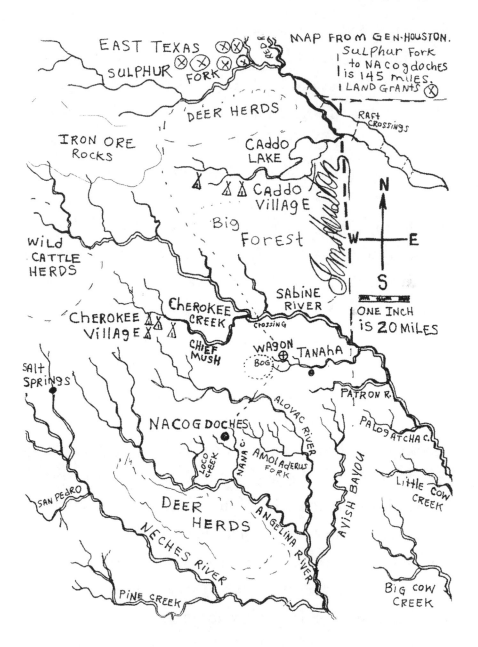

The Consultation of delegates has been in distress with each other. They are to represent their settlements, not strut around like peacocks. The banners will bring more settlers who will be better delegates. We hope to be a new delegate in the future. General Houston seems to be wise as he has a great vision what this land can be. We will do our part to help build this wilderness into something useful! This will be our "New Eden". Our future together is great with a chance to start over with a clean slate. There will be others.

April 8, 1835. We changed into our old clothes before we left Nacogdoches. We thought we saw some men gathered on the road. They went their own way so they have no bone to pick with us. We then rode northeast to the Alovac River. We would camp after crossing the river to let the horses graze on the thick buffalo grass. We know to better pace ourselves to keep from being worn-out getting there. We saw there are many deer signs and wild cattle tracks about. We have seen some wild horses. There are so many great, ancient trees here. We hope that the land is this good on our land grant. My wife fussed at me again because it cost another half dollar to cross at the raft ferry. I feared that we would get stuck in the mud trying to cross the river, so it was worth a full fifty cents. Saving the wear and tear on the team is worth it. Most of all I can't swim. I do not to want to start off on the wrong foot here.

We have camped here for two days due to the rain that has been coming down steady. We picked a high spot to camp on. We tied the wagon secure to a stout tree. We them made the team secured in a grove of trees. There is a small trickle of water close to them where they can drink. We are tired from all this traveling, so we needed to rest for a day. Delephine wants me to pitch a tent since we have been cramped up in the wagon for so long. It is cloudy and the sky grows quite dark since it is the new moon, so I hurry to pitch the tent. Town life has made us spoiled, so we will have to remember a simpler way of living as we did in the past. Still it is nice to know that we enjoyed a few days of living a better life. We have worked hard for years so a few days of fun was warranted.

Tonight, we read: JEREMIAH, Chapter 36, Verse 3. "The Word of God changes you."

There has been so much excitement this past week going to court, and meeting General Houston. With it all going on, there has not been any time to rest, or for fun things to do. I try to plan things out better. Delephine did say, "Take the proper time to get there! We have to be safe and think things out better." I take praise where we can get it. It is hard to stay on her good side sometimes. It is a slippery slope at best. The life in town was nice with a dry roof over your head, fine clothes to wear and food that you did not have to hunt, clean or cook. A body could get fat and happy there,

as it is a much simpler life than we have ever known. I think
about the stores, the hotel, and livery that Mister Goyens
built by trading horses with the Cherokee. Trading horses
seemed better as a money-maker. No matter what happens
with the trade dollar most people still need good horses to
get across these open prairies to the next town. I thought
how it was better than being a dirt farmer when some seasons
you barely just get by with enough to food eat. I did not
realize how much of our life has been sheltered away from
everyone else. Now we have seen more of the world and we
will never be the same. We grew ten years of wisdom in just
a few days. We thought we knew so much about life when
we really know so very little. Every day is brand new with a
chance to start over again.

April 10, 1835. We have been traveling north by east to the
forks of Tanaha Creek. We went around a large bog marked
by some Indian signs on the large stones close to it. The
Cherokee village is now northwest of us by what the map
shows. They are known to be generally friendly and good
horse traders as General Houston and Mister Goyens has
said. Tonight we will settle down early to get a fresh start
tomorrow. We have crossed the second fork of the river to
cross the Sabine by Saturday afternoon, almost one day's ride
in a loaded wagon. We will make good time traveling once we
cross the Sabine. We hear the drums of the powwows during

the night to let us know to keep a safe distance from them. We do this out of respect for their land boundary. They are close by our camp tonight. We made a small fire of mesquite wood to make ourselves not so easy to be seen by the white smoke. We will camp here tonight to cross the river early in the morning. I saw some big campfires of someone who has come here like we have. They are bold to be so careless, so they are not trying to hide, or seek to be hidden from our view. We tried to stay awake and keep watch but we needed some rest from the long road. It is hard to sleep when you are living under the open sky. We watched the falling stars. We wished big wishes. I would not tell her what I wanted most. She knew me well enough to know.

CHAPTER THREE

A Hard Life in Texas.

May 1835. Much has happened since the last month. Today everything has come back to me as if it were a bad dream that I just woke up from. This is what I remember the most of what has happened: We are attacked at night. Not by any Indians, but by strangers that are looking for our valuables, some food, and our horses! They tried to take us hostage. We heard a noise with the horses tied to the willow trees. I went to look after them. So many rifle shots rang out! I went to go for cover to get a shot off at them to scare them off. They are steady shooting at us and they do not back down from a fight. General Houston said that Indians do not like to fight at night for they fear losing their soul in the dark. So it was those people from back at the trading post that attacked us! No one else would know that we had anything much of value. We wore our old clothes, but our new, red painted wagon and nice horses stand out. What could make us ready for anything like this?! I could not know at the time that Delephine was wounded terribly and then she died. She went under the wagon to get a secure spot, out of the line of fire. I was trying to get the horses from being run off and leaving us stranded. She had the good pistol. She emptied it and reloaded back, several times. I tied the horse's reigns to a tree limb. I tried to sneak up on one of them drinking out of a whiskey bottle. I remember that one of them looked like the man from the trading post that loaded our wagon, and another was the man in court at Nacogdoches that was against Mister Goyens! I saw some faces shown up from the muzzle flash as I was so close to them. The fire of the burning wagon showed them up like they are demons from the Devil. They shot us up bad! We have somehow met up with some of the men that likely tracked us all the way from Shreveport thinking that we were some gunrunners to General Sam! I was left for dead as they stood over me and kicked my body to see if any life was left in me! I held my breath and stared a blank look to fool them. I played "possum" so they would have the upper hand. There was no way to know how many there were. The robbers went through the wagon and poured all our goods on the ground. They found some of the silver coins in a flour sack. They poured out all our valuables and spoiled what they could to mock us. It was enough to try to rob us, but then for them to kill us! We would have given them the horses and the money. Our lives mean more than all this trifle!

Our new wagon was caught on fire. They rolled it into the river to sink. There laid my Delephine out in the open and I could not go over to help her. All I could think of was my wife and how brave she was to fight so hard! She lay still on the ground and as soon as they left I pulled myself along the ground until I could put my arms around her. I could not see her face! She was hurt so bad. I was helpless to come to her to do anything about it! I felt my own life fading away. I found a shirt close by so I tried to tie it tight around my chest wound. I lost feeling in my legs as I drug myself to bring her into some low brush. Her body shuddered terribly as life left her. Delephine's soul is not lost because she is a Christian. But she is lost to me now! The other men that remained all left and rode away with our horses, a rifle and a bag of silver. I drug myself next to a burning log because I felt so cold. I lay there wounded just talking to myself. I poured gunpowder into a wound. I got up my courage to take a piece of burning wood to touch it to the worse of my wounds. My skin burned as the wound sealed up. I passed out from pain and the loss of much blood. The men rode off and left their dead among us, to mock us.

A hunting party passed and they saw the fires of the burning wagon that was up to the axles in the water. I heard someone different talking to me. It was a group of Cherokee. One is called Bowles or "Bowl". The other is called something like "Mush". The other is a younger medicine man called Key-Sap. Other Cherokee were there along with one of their elders. They put down their weapons because their hunt was fouled by all the death on their land. They are angry as they shoot many arrows at an old bois d' arc tree. They fire the slain men's guns at this same tree. Their hunt was spoiled by all the blood that was spilled here. I understood that much. They thought that I was crazy because I was talking out of my head by blaming myself. They took off my necklace that the Chitimacha gave me for trade to show that I am a friend. They held it up and showed it to others. These strangers took pity on me as they gave up on their hunt. The younger one took a drum to beat it often as he burned bundles of sage. He took great pride in playing a strong beat on that drum.

The elder Cherokee took a piece of iron from the wagon and put it in the fire. Others held me down as the elder one poured some foul tasting medicine down me. He slapped me hard so I would bite down on a stick. They touched the iron to my back and leg wounds. It sealed them up from me bleeding out like a butchered hog. It hurt so terrible! I knew that death was close if they did not do this quickly. I dreamed about our days back at Nacogdoches; and the other day back when Delephine greeted me so sweetly when I came back empty handed after our cattle were stolen. I thought about Mister Jeremy when we stacked wheat and how he fussed when we felt sorry for him when he was dying. I saw the Widow Lalaurie making a quilt in my daydream. I felt like I was falling back to earth from a long way's away. I came to my senses as my pain came back strong. I could only see out of one eye because my face is so swollen. I felt so weak. It was a wonder that I was alive!

They buried Delephine under that bois d' arc tree after they put cloth over her face and her bonnet on her head to hide her terrible wounds. They placed her pretty dress over her like a shroud. I was too weak to do anything to help bury her. She fought very hard against the robbers. It seems that she shot four robbers as she was shot in a tragic way. I was shot five times! The dirt and bark flew all around me at different times. The gun flashes made it so hard to tell what was going on. My ears still ring from all the shooting. It seems that the Cherokee honored Delephine for being so brave against such great odds. It made me proud for her to be my wife. "She died a good death: worthy of a great warrior! She killed our enemies who might raid our village or be a part of those that would harm us." The one of them named Red Bird speaks some good French and a fair amount of English words. I was not sure if I had imagined it all, like it was a bad dream. They tried to talk with me to keep me from dying right away. At times they seemed to be far away, then like I was sitting beside myself, watching it all. I knew for certain they would not hurt me because these were decent people. Like the Chitimacha, these are real people that do not put on a front. They are just what you see, as they treasure life as being valuable and worth protecting.

They burned the outlaws bodies on a far hill because they did not want their land cursed. Bad people that die are burned so that they will be cursed in the next life, it seems. So this Red Bird did much to explain some important details to me as I try to become stronger and heal. It is still hard to understand what they are saying most days. I do get a few new Cherokee words down as they gesture and make hand signs when they talk. Some others speak a few words of English and French to give me something to relate to. Everyday different ones are teaching me some Cherokee words to understand better what different things are called. They know how to say "eat" or "drink" and "sleep". Now I know the Cherokee words for these same things. Mister Goyens is slated to come soon they have said. They admire him very much because he is considered one of them. I never thought I would be living among these people, but I did like them as they saved me from a terrible death. We never had much family before this day. These people have a strong sense of family. I miss my father and my good wife. They are making sure that I have a good place among their tribe. It felt good to feel important after going through so much grief. They come by to bring me cooked food, fruit and fresh jugs of water. From what I understand I am some kind of good luck for them because I survived the terrible attack from our mutual enemies.

Now that I am stronger they take me to their main camp by being drug on a thing they called a travois. It is made from long pieces of green wood that is tied in a long "X" shape. It has cross bars covered in a blanket where I was secured by a rope. Other people followed closely behind the horse where I would not fall off or be left behind. It was a long trip but we got there in one piece. It wasn't too bad because I am still not strong enough to walk very far. The sun was warm and a slight breeze blew as we traveled along.

The Cherokee of east Texas are quite a large tribe. Their elder medicine man is called San-See. He blessed my wounds again by burning many sage bundles. He said prayers in words I did not understand. He threw salt into the different directions to bless the earth. He continues for several days to give me a strong tea made out of mesquite leaves to kill my bad pain. I felt so weak and sore all over. It is some better after sleeping on and off for almost three days!

William Goyens

I woke up and my head hurt. I wanted some time to read but my close vision is difficult, today.

I am taken down to the river to clean up. I use a walking stick to get about. Some of my clothes are brought to me that they salvaged from our wagon's ruins. Some still fit so I looked better. I found use of a straight razor and a piece of mirror to shave with. I felt much better to improve myself, so this was as good as some stout medicine. There is much noise as a big trade day is going on. The drums are going strong to gather people from the woods and the river. I am excited to have a place here. William Goyens and his oldest son came here with a remuda of ten horses to trade for ten buffalo hides. He made the signs for trade as they set about to bargain with each other. After they finished their trading they shook hands, and smoked a peace pipe together. Chiefs Mush and Bowles asked me to join him in council. Mister Goyens spoke as the interpreter. Chief Mush has many questions to ask, and so do I. William Goyens tells me that he remembered me from our day in court with Judge Ellis B. Thomas. He tried to make me understand what the Cherokee want to know about me. I asked them why they saw fit to save me. They said that their hunt has been bad because of all the raids by the Mexican army. The Sabine smugglers have stolen many of their horses with nothing in trade. A number of women have died in childbirth. So anyone that kills their enemies is their friend. Someone that survives their enemies' wrath is also their allies.

They held out the necklace from the Chitimacha that showed us to be allies. The Cherokee fought battles for the

East Fork trade with the Caddo. So if their enemies admire us, then they do too! It was all very interesting. They told me many things I needed to know better because many things were not so clear to me. Mister Goyens said, "They thought that I was 'William Goyens', or a relative of Goyen's family." I was covered in blood so I could have been anyone. They used the hot iron to close up my terrible wounds. Five of them! I do not remember anything other than I held Delephine for a long while. I managed to drag her farther out into the brush to hide but it was too late to help her. It was most terrible and awful to think of. If they wanted the horses we would let them have them and all our money. All that pales with the loss of Delephine! I have failed her terribly! They told me not to be ashamed or angry. I try to be brave as that is what is expected of me. Red Bird comes to get me to take them to their ceremonial council house. I am so afraid some days.

These Cherokee are meeting in a larger council that has come today to trade horses with William Goyens. It is all of Chief Bowles' and Chief Mushes' tribes that have met here to trade. One is the peace chief, one is the war chief. Around 200 Cherokee here by their councils! They burned sage bundles and they make the smoke signs to tell their plans for today. They brought many wild horses they gathered for trade. They each talked and said their peace. Each one that speaks took a fancy stick called the "talking stick." The person with the stick has the right to talk and when they are finished they pass the stick on to the next person. If someone is rude and troublesome then the stick is used to threaten them until they are quiet and respectful. Even the chief has to hold his peace until the stick is passed. I liked this as it was interesting to see their way of doing things.

Mister Goyens asks me all the questions they want to know. The bigger Cherokee council is wondering about my wife Delephine. "Was she a good wife, or not?" They asked this to see if her spirit is at rest, or does she 'wander' now? Mister Goyens explains it all very carefully so he won't be thought disrespectful. I told Mister Goyens that Delephine was a good wife, and she did not fuss a lot. Mister Goyens explains what I have said. The Cherokees are amused by the answer. Chief Bowles stands and he raises his left arm to curse them. They all get quiet as he speaks in Cherokee. Mister Goyens says that since she was a good faithful wife, then she has earned her good reward. Delephine was buried like a great warrior so she must now be at peace. Her spirit does not "walk" to curse their crops or the hunt. They honored her well with a warrior's burial because she fought so brave against the terrible men. They took away the robber's bodies and burned them on a high hill. He told me many big details that I have a small understanding of. I remembered a good many things but there was much that happened that I was not fully aware of. Since I survived being wounded five times then my scars made me a special person to them. They had me remove my shirt and show them my scars. I pointed to each scar and they yell loudly and beat the drums. Their battle scars are something that they are most proud of. They passed out two baskets of small stones to vote. A white stone means they approve of me. A different stone means they do not like me. A basket is then passed around and they put a small stone in there to vote. The chief's helper pours out the basket on the floor. The majority of the stones are white with just two different colored stones among the many. The chief takes the two different stones and throws them outside the door of the lodge. Cherokee councils shouted their approval of me becoming a member of their tribe. They saved my life and these are good people in my eyes. I thanked them and offered my life back to save them from harm. Red Bird and Mister Goyens spoke on my behalf. They showed their approval to the least of them. The elders threw salt into the air and some shook gourd rattles and blew on bone whistles. The drum bearers played a hearty song that lasted for a while. I felt so honored to have this kind of respect from these strangers. We are no longer strangers because they are my new family. I will fight and die for them if need be. My life belongs to them.

Chief Bowles then asked some warriors do the "Eagle Dance" to give a prayer to the Great Spirit for my wife's safe travel to the next life. This is not how I believe but since they saved me from death I should not offend them. I prayed for Delephine and for these wonderful people who have taken me in as their own. They allowed me a chance to show my respects with my own prayer for her. I spoke some in French. Many know these words from all their trade days. They showed great respect and reverence for when I spoke this way. The Cherokee are sincerely concerned that they may make the evil spirits of the plagues of Smallpox, and Cholera may go past them, to go far away. Chief Bowles trades lead, salt, and iron that is abundant in east Texas. He is often in Shreveport with Mister Goyens to trade new horses. Goyens said that some of the ships from Ireland arrived to New Orleans with these plagues. Anyone that came in contact from these people died. Their ships were burned. So someone from Louisiana who survives a terrible death is a strong influence. Then they think I have some kind a power over what may come their way! I thought it all strange, but we have learned much here. I have never heard of such a thing before this day. Still I must respect them and their beliefs as they would be hurt if I questioned them too harshly over this. They have allowed me to say a good prayer in French for all that have been lost to some disease.

They do not have names, for they number like the stars in the sky as there are too many for us to count.

Red Bird is the younger Medicine Chief. San-See the Elder gave Red Bird advice on the next events to take place to make the spirits not walk. Red Bird got out the drum bearers going to the ridge above the meeting place. The warriors got far into doing the dance. They get going strong after the sun sets. San-See told us that the peace pipe must include all persons in the council, or it will not be a good dance. We took the peace pipe so they would be able to finish their ceremonies. It was not too terrible to be a part of. We did as they asked as they are now my family. Chief Mush said that when your wife is gone, it is not good to be alone. He welcomes me to stay with them to prosper living among them. I am their good luck because I survived the terrible attack. Their hunt has been bad for months. Some of their young women have recently died in childbirth. I am welcome to be a part of their tribe since I have no tribe. William Goyens gives me the official welcome to the tribe. He tells me a great deal I did not know. "They plan to marry you off soon. They said that you have a fierce spirit like a puma. They said that the tribe wants to stay strong." I said, "I am pleased to belong." These people are wonderful.

They are anything but "savages". They have a clear sense of purpose in all that they do.

A big ceremony is followed by a feast that lasted for a day. I will learn to hunt with them. I will help protect them from harm, like they did for me. It is the least I can do. A man has to do what he can to make the people around him feel safe. It is to his benefit to help his tribe to be well and safe. The elders give me much advice and they bring me small gifts of fried cornbread and wood for my fire. We sit together and enjoy the evening together. They show me many different weapons and how they are made so well. They flaked out some nice flints that were baked close to some coals. Bundles of willow shoots are made into some decent arrows. They liked that I was so careful preparing them by removing the bark. They are tied ten to a bundle to dry for a week. I noticed all the small details so well. The arrows are made of willow or dogwood shoots which are soft wood that grows fast and straight. Their hunting bows are made from bois d' arc shoots which grows very slowly over a number of many years. It is a hardwood that is common in this area. I know this wood because we made many fence posts from it in the past. We called it "ironwood" because it turns hard like iron when it gets cured out well. They have me making a good hunting bow from a nice shoot that Red Bird cut for me. It made my hands turn orange

The Escape from Eden

and I got a big thorn in my hand. They usually cut this wood in the winter while the sap is down, but time is short to learn what I need to know. I trimmed it up nice with a big-bladed knife and an old spoke shaver. We soaked it into the river for a day. I had to dig a hole and bury the bow so it would have a nice bend to it as it seasons out good. The stakes in the ground kept it with the proper bend to it. It was a great deal of work but it will be a nice weapon when it is complete in a few months.

June 1, 1835. Mister Goyens told me what day it was. Things have been so curious most days. He is often here to help out with what the tribe needs as far as goods and needs. I am stronger now so it is time to begin to learn to hunt with a bow rather than a gun since they make too much noise and scare off all the game. Bullets, shot and powder are hard to come by sometimes. They are not the true mark of a good hunter, Red Bird has said. I am given instruction to the 'rights and wrongs' in shooting at game. Besides being downwind from a deer, I am covered with a deer hide tied under the chin and around the waist, to secure it. Our faces are covered with colors of earth clays to help hide against the ground. I feel stupid but it is how things are done here. We went up and the deer has been boxed in against a ravine. I aimed and shot. The deer heard the twang of the bowstring and jumped out of the path of the arrow.

The men hiding in the blinds laugh then they grow silent to make quiet signs to each other. The deer jumped over the ravine like it was not there. It was gone in the brush in a moment. We know that there are others that are drawn to the musk scent that has been placed in the trap. Red Bird motioned that we both are to shoot together as a team, to get a single deer. We stay still for about an hour, and up comes a big healthy buck. We both took aim so we drew, and fell a deer by working together. Chief Bowles looked down, and judged that my arrow was the one that best killed the deer. "Being hungry improves your aim!" Red Bird said this in French, then in English. This makes me worthy to be a part of the regular hunt. They give me the initiation of having to eat the fresh liver of the deer. They laugh at me being squeamish to eat it raw, still warm from the deer. I am now more a part of this tribe. I hope that we cook more of the deer, next time! It is a good experience for me to learn more about my new tribe. They are proud of me as we carry the deer back. The elders praise me and pat me on the back as I am in their good graces. Even the elder women bring me wood for my campfire. The deer hide will be scraped good and hung in my lodge as a trophy. The deer skull will be put on a lodge pole.

June 18. It is getting close to the ceremonial time of the Rain Dance. The summer rain is what we need to get us through the hot months to follow. There is a building needed for storage of meat to keep it from spoiling, or being eaten by the coyotes that are so fierce this year. We survey a hill that we can dig part of it out to make into a good storage room, or corn crib. We dig with some stone axes like they are like a hoe. We make little progress with digging. I remember that there are many tools in our wagon at Tanaha Creek. I want to go there again to get the tools from that tool box. Then we get the silver in the wood box and water barrel. The Cherokee asked why I had them hide the water barrel in the water before we left to the Cherokee camp. Now I will go back there with Red Bird to the wagon because there is quicksand along that part of the river. We take two extra horses to bring back the tools, and in case one horse goes lame. We go along Cherokee Creek so we will be there by tomorrow afternoon. We have not seen any other persons so it is good to have Red Bird along as scout, and company. We understand each other better since William Goyens has established our understanding of each other.

Red Bird is a good-natured person to be so patient to teach me so much. I thought that I knew a lot, but not as much as I thought! He is always teaching me something about hunting, and medicine. We make good time down the sandy trail. The horses stop occasionally to graze, and this time lets us stretch our legs. We stop and see rabbit signs. Red Bird picks up a rock and he makes the quiet signs. He stands still, lets out his breath slowly and tosses the rock to kill a rabbit for dinner. Red Bird then points to a rock for me to pick up to try what he just showed me. I got a fair sized rock that I held from the underside. We spotted a good-sized swamp rabbit. I gave it a hard toss as Red Bird has done.

We both will be having rabbit this evening. Red Bird took the hides and turned them skin side up, and poured salt out of a pouch unto the hides. He then placed them, rolled up, into a tree limb, to let the water drain out of them, so they can be scraped of any flesh. They will now be fresh and new smelling. He then took a green limb and I removed the leaves. He made a hoop to stretch hides on. He put them on the same hoop, with the fur side in, opposite each other. He then sews loops of sinew to stretch the hide tight. Our lessons are small, but our learning is great.

Several other Cherokee met us to camp here. They stay back from here in case we need help coming back. An elder took his time to show me where to make a camp from a few tree limbs leaned together for shelter. They show how to make a proper fire with less wood using a piece of flint. At dusk we have made a proper shelter, a good fire with something to eat. This was to get us ready for when time is short and much has to be done. We rested for we will have a big day when the sun comes up. I was ready to get to Delephine's burial place, but that is not how things are done here. We do as the elders tell us to do. One more day passing gets us ready for what we must do to survive here. Morning comes and we get the horses ready to go. The elders have us eat the dried meat that we packed in our goods for the next few days. We can only drink from the water we have in our gourds that are used like a canteen. That is enough to get us ready for the big day. There is some reasoning in what they do here. We are to get the tools from the wagon then I get to go visit Delephine's grave. That seems backwards but they have different ways of doing things.

The wagon is at the next hill. I see the boulder with the Indian signs painted on them. And then I see the tall stand of trees. I am ready to get there soon. We find ourselves there, and we set about to get the tools that we are after. We came to the bend in the river, and all we could see of the wagon is the top of the brake handle. We took our shoes off because the mud would pull off our shoes, and they will be lost. We took the water barrel over in the shallows to get some of the silver stowed away, safely. We broke the barrel hoop to use for a pry bar to open the wood box. The tools and the rest of the silver are there, just as it was left. We got the things removed from the wagon, and we are covered with mud from head to toe. We end up in a mud fight, and all you can see is our eyes. The rest of us is just mud! We both laugh because we are quite a sight! We get cleaned up from our mud fight. It was good to visit here and not be sad. I think that they want me to be able to deal with death better as they have seen much death as they traveled south to live in Texas. Louisiana was not any kinder to us. Life is tough. We have to be ready for what comes our way.

The sun gets past the noon mark. We see that time is short. I found my old axe lying on the ground. We got busy cutting some saplings. We make a travois of green tree limbs to carry the tools back safely. We look for a place above the flood line to bury some of the money. We found a cleft in the rock that would be dry, and secure. We took a bag of silver dollars out for our needs. The rest is put away for later. The Calendar Tree is in line with the silver. Ten paces south of the afternoon shadow of the tree. The tree is an ancient one, with all the bark removed. There are signs on the trunk burned in with a fire stick. The tribes hold a council here one time a year, the most important event of the year is marked there by being burned into the tree. Red Bird said that this is a good place to hide something, in an open place. We covered the silver with a large rock, and smaller stones, and sand. It is now well covered. We can now head back so I can visit Delephine's grave.

I tell Red Bird that I want some time alone to visit my wife's grave as the sun is getting low in the sky. Red Bird pointed out the place where she is buried up on a high ridge. This way she is honored as a fierce warrior that killed four fierce enemies of the Cherokee tribe. There is a bois d' arc tree with two hanging cow skulls painted with sun signs and lightning. It has turkey and eagle feathers hanging down from long strings. There are many arrow points and rifle balls shot into the tree trunk of the ancient tree. This is a tree that many of their hunting bows came from. There is a gun from an enemy tied to a high tree limb. He then left me alone to pay my respects until it gets dark. I spent over an hour there paying my respects. I prayed and laid face down as it all comes back to me what all has happened. Red Bird whistles as he stands on the edge of the grove where my Delephine is buried. He does not like death or burials because he is a healer from what I can see. He stands back and away from me. He has burned a small fire with sage bundles as I prayed on the hill top. He motions for me to get the horses. He says something in Cherokee, then in French and English. He knows so much! I understand many of their words better. He takes out two drums and we play them with a stick to play a song he sings. The sun sets as the drums continue on strong. He pats me on the back and he praises me for keeping up well in my drumming. He says, "We celebrate the good things our loved ones gave us, to carry them with us the rest of our lives." I liked that. I did not sing. Delephine would have liked that too. She always put her fingers in her ears, because my singing is so terrible. I thought about that and told my brother. He laughed and told me that I am crazy. From now on this will be a place of celebration, not death. Things have changed.

We take our horses and a travois to head back to Cherokee Creek, and our summer village. Now we have some real tools: three long-handled hoes, a good saw, two shovels, a grubbing axe, and two double axes. Some like these could be bought in Nacogdoches, but these are special tools because of the great sacrifice that came to bring them here. These make our work that much more hearty and useful because of what these items represent to me. I can still build a life here in Texas, and that would be what Delephine would want me to do. There is now a chance to make some real progress in our building plans. These tools will make us prosper as we can do so much to make our tribe better with some lodges, a council house and a secure corn crib.

We get back safe and the elders welcome us and they look at what we bring back from our trip to the wagon. I made some time to draw on the ground with a stick to show them my ideas for their village improvements. We can make the meat storage room, and whatever they want. We got permission to cut some trees. One tree comes from here, one from there, and some broken limbs from the recent storm. Not to all come from the same place the elders of our tribe have said. This makes it harder to do, but it keeps the woods full, and helps hide the village from the hot sun. There are a lot of helpers. I took the double axe, and showed a young warrior how to make a notch out of the trunk, and to chop on the opposite side to make it fall where you want it to. There are plenty of helpers. The young children are watching some of the trees fall. They follow the men back and forth, taking them a gourd full of water to drink, between the long trips to carry cut trees. They carry small limbs that break off the trees. Copying the movements of the men teach them more about life, in their play. This is how they learn of the world: even their play involves the hunt, or something that helps them to be aware to work together. Everyone has a job to do and all contribute to the wellbeing of the tribe or they are run off or punished if they go out of their way to do wrong. The sticker patch is no place to be put for a long day in the hot sun.

June 21. This is the summer solstice, the longest day of the year. There is much to do. All building stops for a few days to make time for their important ceremonies. The elders get the dancers ready so that the Rain Dance, and the Green Corn Dance, for the girls who are now young maidens. There is also the Jimson Weed Dance where all the single people are matched up into couples. This is one that I have heard so much from Mister Goyens. Now they are going to marry me off. I have mixed feelings about anyone else but my wife. We have settled the fact that she is resting safe and secure. That seems to warrant that I should choose one of these maidens for myself. I have mixed feelings about what I should do. It has been very lonely without someone to help me and take care of me. I will just participate in their ceremonies to see what happens next. The Green Corn Dance is done first. The younger maidens have been preparing for a week to show off for the tribe today. They are young women now, dressed in their best clothes. Their face is painted with corn pollen, and earth clays to represent their change from being a girl to a woman.

The corn dancers are presented to the tribe. They look quite lovely so the elders give their nod of approval to the maidens. They are marched two times around the camp, east to west to show them off, and wish them a long life. They are now given new names to be called by. They may keep their old name if they choose to, but most like the status of being considered an adult, so the new name reflects that. Chief Bowles calls them by their new names. The tribe cheers for each one like they were the last Cherokee on earth. They beat drums, shake rattles and shout like thunder. Each woman is given small presents from the tribe. The maidens have walked around where we sit on the southern field close to the camp. These young girls will be matched with a young man for a future time. This gives them a chance to get to know each other in the coming year. They will marry this time next year.

The Rain Dance starts. All the dancers are dressed to the teeth, paint and all. They dance in different groups until it is late evening. We are getting hungry, but the feast will not be ready until after the Jimson Weed dance. The Jimson Weed dance is about to start. Chief Mush asks all the single men to come to the field east of them. Red Bird points to me to go. I go, but I am still dragging my feet. They are urging me to go because it is not good for a man to live alone. I go. The men are sent to one spot in an open grove of oaks.

The single, older women are sent to circle about the camp, much like the maidens have done earlier. The men sit on the ground, and try not to act interested or nervous. The maidens stand in a straight line going north and south. The maidens take slow careful steps, like they are out hunting. They circle the group of men twice for the ladies to get a look at all the single men. The women put their hands up to their eyebrows to block the glare of the sun. She looks to the left then the right. As a woman passes a man that she likes, she gives him a present. Several women have passed and given their present to a man of their choice. If he accepts, he stands holding the small gift that she has made for him. She then stands beside him and looks very happy to be considered worthy. There is a woman that has walked past several times almost too shy to pass. I am presented a small leather tobacco pouch with some beadwork in the shape of a Cherokee star on it. It is a fine gift from a lovely woman named Say-te-Qua, or Morning Star. She is Chief Mush's daughter so I would not refuse her gift. She is most proud when I stood to say that I accept her gift. So she will be my future bride. The tribe yells their approval at each match. They yell very loud at Say-te-Qua because she is the chief's elder daughter.

She has to be married before anyone else can. She was to
marry before but her perspective husband died so she stayed

single for a long while. The tribe will prosper and be complete now. I will soon be a new husband. Tonight, I am tired but I cannot sleep. I know I am doing the right thing by marrying this Cherokee woman. She is quite lovely and wonderful. I do not know what see sees in me, but she must see something. She is nice, but I do not know if it is too soon to marry her, or anyone for that matter. It might be a mistake not to, since her people have saved my life. I do owe them my life. My own life would have been lost had they not found me and healed me from my wounds. I want to stay here for my land grant would be useless to me now. Red Bird could not sleep either. He must be just as scared as I am, for he is to be wed to Ke-Ke. She is a busy bee into everything under the sun. I tried my best to encourage Red Bird. We were both nervous knowing that our bachelor days are soon coming to an end. He tried to explain that we had to go through some rituals that I did not understand very well. So far they have been very generous to me. They allowed me some room to do some things to help the tribe showing that I would make a good member. I just wanted to fit in for I feel that here is where the Lord wants me to be. He would not have placed me here for some good reason. The crickets sang all night. The frogs croaked along with them. One was in my bedroll and it went down my shirt. I ran outside the lodge jumping around trying to be free of the frog. People came out of their lodges to see what the noise was all about. Red Bird shook his head, and pushed me into the creek fixing my problem. I think that he put that frog down my shirt when I was asleep. Some elders came out of their lodge to see what was wrong. Red Bird laughed and he told them that I was going for a swim to calm my nerves. He is laughing at me for being so crazy. Getting the attention of the elders was not good to do because there is so much going on. They are tired so their patience is short. The Elders help to make sure all things are done properly.

I am calm and collected now after my late night swim. I found a blanket and got warm by the fire. The rest of the night was peaceful. Red Bird could not sleep. He gave me a piece of corn cake so I took part of it to eat. I was over the frog and now after my swim, I am sleepy. I will pray over what I should do about my future. I feel that I am to marry Chief Mush's daughter. That is that. I will read some to try to make my eyes tired so I can sleep. I have much to think about. My eyesight is better these days.

Tonight, before I sleep I read the Bible that I have in my pack. I feel that I have a lot to think about so it is good to seek refuge in the words.

Revelation Chapter 2, verse 28."And I will give him the Morning Star."

CHAPTER FOUR

Becoming a Good Cherokee.

I have slept a few hours and woke up at sunrise. I walked around to think about my about my future with the Cherokee. The camp dogs were very playful. I threw a stick and the dog would fetch it back to me. Some of the children came out of a lodge under the watchful eyes of the women who were getting the fires started for the cooking pots. The children played with the dogs and they brought out a few leather lacrosse balls. They had them going strong chasing them around. Earlier I was wondering if it was the right thing to marry this Cherokee woman. Now seeing these fine children has made me realize that I was making the right decision to marry her. Delephine would approve. She would not want me to be alone the rest of my life. These are my new family, these great Cherokee! I am learning to speak more of my words better. I still have Red Bird close by to correct my mistakes so I do not put my foot in my mouth in front of the whole tribe. So far I have managed not to do that, so I will step carefully in my words and deeds. Things sure have changed from the days we farmed in Flatwoods! I would have never dreamed that I would be living here with these people. They have been generous and kind to me as a stranger. They treat me as part of their tribe and as if we have the same blood. They are generous to give me back my life. I owe them everything I have because my life would be lost like Delephine was lost to me.

Red Bird asked me to talk with him. He is marrying Ke-Ke, who is Say-te-Qua's younger cousin. He wants me to give him advice about marrying her. My advice isn't worth two jujus. I just said we have honor our choices for it would be terrible to go back on your word. We would be run out of the tribe if we had changed our minds. If I let him run out on his promise, then they would put me out in the sticker patch like they do to thieves or liars. Case closed. He told me that the Cherokee came from the Carolinas to make east Texas their new home. The tribe must stay strong. It may not make for a healthy future if Red Bird disappointed them. He understood me just fine. Even in my most terrible use of the Cherokee tongue. He was able to put some sense from that. He laughed at my choice of words like a good brother would.

He corrected me on a few things. It is nice to have a brother as I have never had one before now. We were making plans to build their new council house here. Red Bird has seen a good one that the Caddo made. He took a stick and drew what it looked like in the dirt. It is round shaped and plenty roomy. He walked to a circle of cedars. We cut off the main limbs to expose the trunks. We then cut around the bottom around the trunk to make the tree not come back out. He called this kind of building "poteaux en terre"-post in the ground. These cedars are well rooted so he makes good use of them. They make a circle that is 40 feet in diameter like a big wagon wheel. We have plenty of wood from the recent storm to make good cross beams from. We have some young braves helping us. They were good help and they have a good idea on how to finish this out.

Black Bear, Chief Mush's helper came to ask us to stop this job for the much needed corn crib. I took back the tools I needed to get started. It seems since I brought the tools everyone has their own projects to use them for. I had to borrow the bigger grubbing hoe back with the promise that it could be used again after tomorrow. I had a good-sized hole dug out of the hill in no time. I found little stone for a change until I had dug down 4 feet deep. Then it was tough going. I managed to chip out a good-sized piece of white stone. Red Bird helped me pry it loose. I went to see if there was any more stone that was lose. There was a great deal of clay here. Red Bird got the elder women to come dig it out for pottery use. I thought of Delephine and the Chitimacha women making their wonderful pots. These women are just as serious as they work making those coils into pots. They can really make some fancy clay baskets in a short time. The women came in there and they dug out all the good red clay into some reed baskets. They sit a short ways away to start making a few things as they have some sand to add to it. The rich clay is worth the effort to mine it, so they dug as much as they can. This gave me a chance to catch my breath and drink several gourds full of water. Many corn cakes were brought to us to eat. I never want to offend someone's good cooking. I enjoyed several of them as different women offered them to me. The wind picked up so it was nice. Working outside was fun with so many helpers.

The sun grew low in the sky. It was time to rest and get cleaned up good at the river. Up walks the chief's helper Black Bear to talk with me. He told me to come to the chief's lodge. I hurry to go there as you don't make the chief wait too long. I tried to get cleaned up and find a change of clothes since this is important to talk with the chief on some important business.

Chief Mush stands outside his lodge with his arms crossed. He wears a different headdress than most, because he is the war chief. He signs for me to have council with him. We then go outside his teepee to talk, in a circle of stones. He tells me that I will catch two horses. I will bring them and tie them to the lodge pole outside his home by the time of the full moon which is two weeks away. I thank him in my best use of Cherokee words. He tells me in English that he has heard "much good" about me. It seems that they speak a number of tongues here from their trade with many different people. I have struggled to just speak some decent Cherokee words to them. So they have understood me many times when I spoke outright! I failed in my speech and my actions. They probably think I am a fool half the time. I do my best and that is all I can do. He offers me a good rope, a jug of water and an ear of corn to eat off of while I go hunting.

Two days have passed and I have not caught any horses. I could not even catch old Radish at this rate! My brother Red Bird gives me some good advice to tell me to not try so hard. Horses can sense that someone is angry or scared so this puts them off from coming close to us. We go out to rope some horses, only to rope some bushes. I will keep trying. Red Bird hides in the brush and he manages to get a young colt captured. He puts him in a small brush corral he made from brush, stones, and a few logs I helped him move. The colt whinnies and it draws a mare and another colt closer. He points me to a gray Appaloosa as it gets close to my hiding place. I rope it. I pull the rope tight. The horse looks startled and it runs with me holding on with all my might. It drags me through the brush, the bull nettles and the briars. It headed through the cactus patch and stopped. I still did not let go. I held on until it tired out. It has drug all the hide off me. I was not going home empty handed! What a man does for the love of a good woman! The next one I catch will be a far gentler horse. We put them with the other horses in the brush arbor we made. This attracted other horses from the area. I found a sorrel with a white star on her blaze. This is a worthy gift to a father-in-law. I place both horses in front of Chief Mush. He accepts them and ties them to the lodge pole. The elders look at the horses and they approve of the gift. They look me over to see how battered and bruised I am. They marvel that I have no broken limbs as some would expect. The marriage of Say-te-Qua is on. Ke-Ke is speechless for once! Marvels never cease. Red Bird caught his horses with less trouble than I have. Red Bird has made his father-in-law Chief Bowles happy. He has plans for the future: a goal of a big family with his horses growing in numbers. Now we are in good terms with our future new family members.

We understand our importance to the Cherokee here. I have our own lodge, next to the chief. We enjoy having the help of the council to do projects that benefit the tribe. The elders' council has made plans on the new smoke house where we can cure the meat from a good hunt. The heat will beat soon that the summer months are half over. We get the word of more settlers coming here soon. The Mexican land grants are in big trouble. They are losing their influence with the new settlers. We are building up our own defenses by making a watch tower on a high hill. It is like I saw at Baton Rouge at the old fort there. The elders fear that more outlaws are coming here to raid like the Mexican army has done in the south of Texas. Word has come from some Cherokee men that worked in a salt mine by Victoria. The Mexicans have lost their leader Maximillian. Red Bird said this Santa Anna has taken over their government and they have cut their horse trade to us. They owed much money in the past and promised good trade to us. Now they take many horses, scouts, and crops and give nothing back so we are at war with the bold Mexicans in their fancy uniforms. They will have trouble sneaking up on us. I told Red Bird, "If anyone comes after us then we will get that Ke-Ke after them!" He laughs so we move on to do some hunting.

Wild cows have been tearing up the milpas of corn, so that lead cow is set for our dinner table soon. We go out in the corn patch with ourselves hidden by some corn stalks tied to our heads. We hold some arrows in our teeth so we make a good aim and rid ourselves of the troublesome cow. The other cows leave out since their leader is gone. I took off my corn stalks cover because it itches so much. We call on the others to come and take the cow away to butcher it away from the cornfield since it would draw other animals if too much blood is spent here. They offer us the heart but we offer it to the elders to make their hearts stronger. We give the liver to an elder woman and she dances around as a fresh liver ranks up there with honey to some folks.

Red Bird makes rawhide shields from the cowhide. He then paints it with charcoal mixed with animal fat. He draws the Rain Bird Spirit, the person or spirit that brings the rain. He then draws a picture of a badger, the sign of the south, to place in his tepee. He patched the hole where the rain comes in. A rain bird is the sign of the separate nature of men and women and healing. North is the mountain lion. South is the badger. East is the wolf. West is the sign of the bear. All this is news to me, but it is important to know all this. The colors mean the different directions: north is white, south is blue, east is red, and west is black. When I see black and white signs painted on the rocks then I know to go to the northwest to find the camp or hunting party. I want to know this Say-te-Qua much better. We all stay busy during the day on our building project. The tribe is growing fast with the Cherokee that have come here this month. It is more people that we have room for. We can't build that much here so we may have to move to the new campgrounds east of here. This land where we are camping floods too much so we will move the village to higher ground. Either way I can be useful to the tribe for planned notions.

It is evening. Say-te-Qua brings some food to me where I am resting. She brings a large gourd full of cool water for me to drink. She wants to show me that she is a good caretaker so this means that she will be a good wife. Right now I can only see her in the daylight. If I see her past sundown then one of these elder ladies said that she would use a tree stump on me! I did not wish to find out any more than that! I am sure that she means what she said. So I will only speak to her when she has another person with her in the daylight. Ke-Ke is usually besides her talking in a fast trot. Her name means Happy Bird. So the word for "bird" and the word for "happy" are the same Cherokee word. She is a chirpy little outfit, so they named her well. They come here to check out my work here in the corncrib. They are trying to hide, but not very well. They watch all that we do and they talk between themselves and they laugh like young girls do. I don't mind because they are sweet women and they are most beautiful. It is easy to spot them close by. They are watching me and Red Bird work. Red Bird tells me about her so I can understand her better and know how to best deal with her properly. I went to draw her face. She said, "No!"

Say-te-Qua is the dream interpreter of the tribe. She tells of the hunt: when it is good, and when it is bad. The chief's dreams are told to her. She gives him council to what it means, and in matters of war. She holds a high place in the council. Say-te-Qua has more "say-so" than most women do. She watches me work during the day. I do not stop to talk as she watches me work. I want to be a good member of the tribe. All I can think about are her big brown eyes and her laugh. I think about that mean old Ogre Woman ready to hit me with a big tree stump. Then I get back to working! An old woman can be meaner than a bear poked with a sharp stick. Who wants to find out what this really means?

The Cherokee elders decide to stay here in this campsite for this next season. We are to keep with the notion of building a much larger council house like the Caddo's have. We found a nicer grove of cedar trees to top off. We cut around the tree trunks to keep the trees from coming back out. Some of the younger tribe used the axe to cut and remove the limbs off the standing tree trunks. I let them help as everyone has a job to do here because we can't do it all by ourselves. We now have a sturdy post to build on the roof of reeds laid end to end. There is a window flap made of reeds made into a mat. This will keep it dry on cool on the west side of the lodge. I remember many of the details I saw back in Louisiana with the Caddo in their lodges and council house. The days go by quickly with our building notions. I have helped pick up two baskets of smooth river stones for the floor. It keeps the weeds out. In cold weather the fire makes the stones warm to the feet. The little things make you live more comfortable. The older women pack clay into the bottom of the fire pit. The hearth is two feet wide, and four feet long. We have dug it two feet deep so that they can pack it with some wet clay to make it a good base for the fire. We placed the river stones on their narrow ends to make sure that the ashes will not blow out if the wind kicks up. The fire hole in the roof has a piece of a canvas tent to put over the hole if the rain is too bad. We took some rope and tied each end to a heavy stone for a weight to keep the wind from blowing it away. This will make it dry and secure when we need it the most.

I have been so busy that I have not set the date when we will marry. Ke-Ke came by and gave me a friendly reminder that she could throw a stump herself. If she cannot do it, she knows an old woman who can! I laughed and she looked very serious at me. Red Bird thinks that I should set a date before I have to tangle with this Ogre Woman. This witch seems to be invisible, but she can appear out of nowhere. She can put the hurt on you! The women of this tribe know how to put the fear of the spirits against you. Since I have worked so hard I am not to be left out in the cold. Ke-Ke said that she cannot marry until her elder cousin Say-te-Qua marries. She said, "Please hurry before I embarrass her in front of the tribe by waiting too long." She has a certain husband in mind for herself: Red Bird, the young medicine chief. It could not happen to a better man. His life will never be the same! It is much better that he marries her than it would be for me. I could not keep up with her. She is a good wife for him and not for me. She is a good woman. I would not get along with her too well. She bosses too much for my liking.

Tonight, I read: Luke Chapter 13, "The Parable of the fig tree in the vineyard."

Today, Red Bird and I went out to hunt some deer. We found plenty of tracks and deer signs but no deer to bring home. We then found some deer at close to dusk. I shot at a buck and missed it. He got a doe to bring back home. We were helped to carry it to camp, which was appreciated. They built a big fire and it was cooked well in a few hours. My stomach growls as you can't eat a day before the hunt. A jackrabbit would cook faster, but it would not feed so many as this. Red Bird gave me the credit for killing it which was not true. He was the person with the great aim, not me. The horns were taken off. I placed them in the tree close by the lodge as a trophy to be well remembered. It was my first real hunt since I have been here. The elders took note of the deer we brought in. We had a big feast and we were asked to tell how we hunted the deer. The elders were amused at our story that we told with Red Bird telling how well I hid in the brush waiting for the deer to come closer for a good shot at it. He is a better storyteller than I am. So I let him do most of the talking. He then tells the story of the grey horse dragging me through the briars and the sticker patch. I stand up to stop him. He laughs and holds me back to keep talking. They laugh because we are now brothers that get along well enough to joke with each other.

The chiefs both stand and they praise us for getting along so well. Chief Mush takes a knife and cuts the tip of my right thumb. He then slightly cuts Red Bird the same way. We have to touch our cut thumbs together to make us blood brothers. They are held together for a moment and our hands are tied loosely with a leather thong. I am responsible for Red Bird, and Red Bird is responsible for me as two brothers that are Cherokee. We are like David and Jonathan in the Bible. We are from different mothers, but we are brothers for life. I want to do more to help the tribe prosper here in east Texas. I would have never guessed that they people would want me as a part of their tribe. This is where the Lord wants me to be, so I must always do my best.

Tonight I read First Samuel Chapter 20. "David and Jonathan."

I went today to tell Say-te-Qua that I am ready to be wed. I have been getting so much attention since I came here. She was relieved that I had not disgraced her in front of the tribe. Making the chief's daughter mad still may not be a good idea, so I set about to make things right and proper between us. Ke-Ke was giving Red Bird some difficulty because he was trying to keep up with her. I wished him luck on that. She walks at a full gallop with her mouth always somewhere close behind! She is a good person, a good woman. Red Bird made some progress with her so we were soon to be close family.

Tonight, we read: Romans Chapter 6, verse 3. "Newness of life."

July 25, 1835- We are both given consideration at the regular council that meets at the new moon. They agree that we need to wed soon. They offer up jokes about the Ogre Woman. Both Chief Mush and Bowles stand together. Black Bear brings out a decorated walking stick. He holds it up high and waves it around. All the talking stops since they get all our attention. He holds the talking stick that means that he cannot be interrupted until he passes the stick to the next speaker. He says his peace to all. Anyone who interrupts will have the talking stick used against them. I get the message. The single people are to be joined together at the dark of the moon. The two sweat lodges need to be built to get us ready to be joined together in the Cherokee style. Two lodges are each set at opposite ends of the camp to give privacy. The men are in the north end of the camp marked by the sign of the mountain lion, or puma, the name that they proudly call me by. The women's lodge has the sign of the buffalo with a shield handing over their lodge.

The Elders mind the space between the two sweat lodges. They control who is helping do the important tasks. They keep the noisy and busy bodies from keeping them from making more progress. We are under their constant watch. They soon have the sweat lodges ready for us. We are not allowed to work on our own sweat lodge for it is considered bad luck. They said that we will have many sweat lodges to build and this is our time to fast and drink lots of water to clean out our body during the sweat lodge. They wish us well. I have to stand out in the hot sun and my hands are tied with a thong of leather to a tree. San-See then takes a green bull nettle and brushes them slowly over my arms. I am not allowed to speak or act like I hurt. He then waits until the heat makes the nettle stings much more painful. San-See says, "This proves that you are willing to suffer for your tribe. You must be willing to do what we ask, without question." We do as he asks to make sure we become a good tribe member. San-See then undoes the ties on my hands and puts my arms in some warm water that has dried bull nettle set into it. This makes pain go away.

The bull nettle was put in boiling water then it is cooled. He brushed against our arms and legs using a cattail. It still felt like a hornet's sting for the rest of the day.

The sweat lodge is done next. We have fasted and been separated into two groups. The women are sent to their trials as we go to our own lodge. It is hot and a little scary. The elder medicine chief is San-See. He talks to us all about our future as husbands and our responsibilities to keep the tribe strong. Red Bird said, "I am ready to settle down and start making plans. Our lives will never be the same: the Bad Ogre Woman is your mother-in-law if you cross the line somewhere!" We talk about our big plans. The elder men tell us of the great responsibility to our family and tribe. We have learned a great deal. I sweated until I am ready to pass out. They drag us outside the sweat lodge to throw us into the spring water. It is cold even in the summer time. We are now freezing cold. They hand us a buffalo robe. On the other end of the camp are the women. I hope that they are faring better than I am. Red Bird and I are both going to marry women close as sisters. Red Bird panics for the first time as he is out of his head. He tries to find a horse to leave out. The other men hold him back and they pull him off his horse. I talk to him. He says that he is just nervous. It is understandable for we are in the same boat. I am doing better now and so is he. We sit by a small fire to rest until the morning. We are given much water to drink because we have sweated so much. We woke at sunrise to get things ready. I wanted to draw a picture of my brother, but he is against it.

Friends have given us cotton-cloth wedding shirts with painted designs on them for good luck. We accepted them and gave a rope of tobacco to say thanks to the giver. A gift requires a gift to be given in return. The councils assemble as we get dressed up in our nice shirts and clothes. We are ready to move on. We know that the ladies must be lovely and ready after what they must have been through. The women walk out to where we are and the tribe cheers as they walk up to us. Chief Bowles praises us for the corncrib and council house that we made and that we are "good Cherokees" in the sight of the tribe. We stood on one side of the stream, and the women stood on the other side. The young children sat on a large tree limb, where they can see the events of the wedding. San-see stands on the east side of the spring, and throws salt in the air to each of the directions. San-See then says a prayer of blessing. All of us are then brought into the stream knee deep in the cold water.

Red Bird and Ke-Ke are wed first. Red Bird was brave as he mustered his courage. He was blessed by San-See. He asked the men here to line up in place with their intended bride. We have been ready for a good celebration today!

The best are saved for last. We are joined together holding hands in the middle of a spring. We will enjoy the river of life together. San-See announces that we are wed to the tribe. They all yell to make animal noises, something that I could never do. We are now welcomed by the elders to a feast in our honor. We ask the elders to eat first. They said that the young married couples are to eat first. Then they will eat according to tradition. We eat for the first time in a day. Happily all the talking and well wishes are for us. We are now happy to be together without the threat of the Ogre Woman! I can no longer fear tree stumps! It is good not to be alone any more. We go to lodges made for us on a high hill. I have many blessings to be thankful for here! I will make more time to pray for guidance and wisdom.

September 15, 1835. There is rumor of a Cholera epidemic in the San Antonio area. People are in trouble from traveling about drinking bad water too close to where their latrine drains. Strangers do not know to read the warning signs since they speak different languages. People drinking out of a water barrel tend to pour some of it back, to be saving. This may be what is poisoning them with the Typhoid disease too. It is better to pour out any left over water when filling the barrel up. Keep the ladle clean. We try to have good practices so our health will be good. We will stay away from anyone hailing from San Antonio for at least six months. We will not trade with them. William Goyens is due to come here in the new moon to trade horses. He is to be north of there, so he is safe from the threat for the time being.

September 28. Red Bird said that he was going to tell off on me to Mister Goyens about the way that gray horse dragged me through the briars. I still managed to hang on the lasso. He looks very happy. Red Bird is good-natured so he enjoys life every day. Even when there is difficulty he seems to manage to have a positive outlook. He is good to have for a friend. I would not be here if he had not found me wounded. What was once a terrible thing has now become something that made me feel stronger. I see things differently now.

October 1. Say-te-Qua is talking about her plans for a future family. First she wants a boy, then a girl. Then we will decide how many more we want at that time. There is a lot to do. We will want to do our best to keep the number of the tribe strong. I want them all to be healthy and happy so they can help us when we farm. San-see gives us a medicine pouch to wear around our necks to protect us from harm and for us to be fruitful to have many children. I do not believe in this but to disrespect these wonderful people would do harm to our future relationship. That could prove a big mistake for my health and wealth. I owe them a great deal, so that warrants I act and do much better.

I often read the Bible out loud to my wife. She asks me, "What do all these new words mean?" The Cherokee version is more difficult to say, but the thing is that it made a spark of interest in reading. I will teach her to read so she can teach our children to read when they get ready. She will have us some beautiful children when the times are much better.

Tonight, I read Matthew Chapter 12, verses 29-30. "Jonah and the Whale."

October 12. We go out to meet William Goyens and his eldest son. They have brought two young Cherokee to help them move the remuda of horses for the Texican army. General

Houston will soon come here with a few soldiers to help him. The Texican army has promised to leave the Cherokees alone if they stay peaceful as we have been. General Houston wants to make a peace treaty with the Cherokee. The Cherokee live up to their word. A legal paper will help secure their land from being taken under what Mister Goyens named as eminent domain. This way all their land in east Texas will be secured and reserved for only the Cherokee tribe. We just want to be left to raise our families, trade horses, and to live in peace.

The past treaty of Chief Bowles and Maximilian prove that he is peaceful unless provoked for some good reason. He promised good trade between them for horses, salt, and hides. It was about enjoying some good trade relations not any kind of politics. This trade is more valuable than this paper money being traded for goods. Horses hold their value. The value of paper money will vary from week to week due to discounting. It takes 5 of our dollars to make one of theirs. It is hard to trade with them, or take much stock in paper trade. We feel that the treaty will keep us safe in the long run. Our land must be protected. We will trade horses with the Texican army, to profit from all the mustangs that are plentiful along the bayous and ravines.

Mister Goyens said that he would teach us ways to catch more horses, without risking life and limb. Red Bird looked at me, and said nothing. Mister Goyens takes us scouting some horses. He has some Cherokee to start a fire, to coax the horses into a ravine. They are directed along the ravine, to sort the good ones out. Horses are roped from both sides of the ravine to keep them from moving away. A blindfold is placed over the horse's eyes. They are led away to a corral where they are fed and watered. They have a few days to get use to us before we move them. They get to know us by us bringing them hay and oats. We bring out a few at a time from the corral. We then put on a loop around the horse's right rear leg. He is led around the corral the horse is then driven almost up to his neck in deep water, until he learns to obey or drown. It seems rough to the horse but he is wild. His instincts will take over. He will learn before harm would come to him. It was difficult for the first horse, but with their help it has helped me break the first one. I will not be over confident for horses are so unpredictable, especially those greys.

It rained a great deal so we have a big meeting in the council house. Lightning crackled and it poured down to the point of being a flood. The men are being honored for gathering so many horses. We are given a stick that is carved like a horse's head on one end, and the other end is carved like a hoof. Horse hair is tied to it like a mane. Some maidens dance and they take the sticks and hold them up high. The singers come out with the drums going strong. They have a spirited dance to celebrate the new wealth of the tribe. Horses mean great wealth as they can be traded for whatever we need. William Goyens has built half of the businesses in Nacogdoches by his sale of many healthy mustangs. A person has a great reputation and honor as they gain more wealth in the tribe. It is exciting to hear the stories of past adventures. Then I have to get up and tell my own story in my crude use of Cherokee. Red Bird acts it out as they all laugh as they have great respect for me to tease me so. Red Bird does a great show of me trying to remove the stickers I got in my back side. San See laughs very hard. He has been ill and he is much better today. It made me feel good to see him so happy because he is close to 90 years old! They now call me a name that means "Sticker Britches"! They sound off with their approval. They clap and hoot like an owl and make animal noises. They admire my great effort to catch horses because I was such a green horn. I was determined to do right so they like me for who I am. We have a good time together as a large family. It feels good to belong to such wonderful people because now I am one of them. I am loved by them as a cherished member of their tribe. They are well respected by me.

CHAPTER FIVE

The Cherokee Scout for the Texicans

October 5, 1835- General Houston is here with 50 men in need of some horses. He said that he did not have long to talk, for General Cos has been reported to be gathering troops to make raids of horses, and cattle close to Gonzales and San Antonio. We said that we would like to join into the fight to stop any thieving by whoever causes it. We have our own opinions over such things. The General asks us to talk with our chiefs Bowles and Mush to tell them out of courtesy. He must be consulted. The wife has to understand that we will not allow people to come in and take everything that they want without a proper trade or sweating out the labor to get it. Red Bird says that warriors have to answer to each other. Cherokee are not made to fight any battles that they do not want to be a part of. We sent a runner to their camp. They can make it back in a day. We wanted to tell my wife a different way but the circumstances make it important to act in less than a week. She knows how I feel about thieves and those that would harm our tribe.

October 12. More men are coming north of here to meet and train under General Houston. We brought two large of remudas of horses. They will need many fresh horses. They will use all that we brought and still need more. The men have come with 5 members of the Texican army. We have been asked to join the army in the form of a home guard to protect our land from invaders. We will be trained in some warfare, get new weapons, and learn better tactics to help give us the upper hand in battle. The runner that we sent home has returned with an ear full of news. He said that she had a fit, fussed, and stomped around. Then they got mad! This is not how I wanted to tell her. They will have to understand that we will do what we must protect our home. After earlier losing what was promised to be my home. I will not be quick to give up what I have labored for: a family and a secure home. We will start out as a scout and then work our way up higher into the ranks of the army. I prayed to be wise, to be strong and to return home as soon as I can.

December 2, 1835. We will train here two weeks and two months according to General Houston. He says that there are more men to join us coming from the Northern Federal States. There is a bonus of land for all that have joined this army. People are better fighters when they have a stake in things. The course of events will dictate how long the training will be. We are to not fight until we get word to. We are to just get away to better report any invaders to our leaders. Just like in a council with Chief Bowles. Now our chief is General Sam Houston who has the confidence of Chiefs Bowles, and Mush. Arkansas chief Ooh-Lu-Teeka is General Houston's adopted Cherokee father. He talked about him a great deal. Sam Houston lived with the Cherokee before he was twenty. He is almost forty as the head of a largest army south of the Sabine. He has big plans for this land as the big chief. We will fight General Cos for his invasion of Gonzales. He will not be meeting the same easy pickings as their fight at the mining town of Zacatecas. They refused to pay tribute to Santa Anna. He asked for their silver to fund his campaign General Sam told us. They all died fighting. We pay no tribute to anyone else that goes against us. We will fight them to the last man if need be! These are like the people who killed Delephine and tried to hurt me! No one is going to push us around now! We now have more of a solid army backing us. Alone we are nothing. Together we are a force to be reckoned with! Now there is a chance to fight on an even field. We are not alone trying to be like little David against the giant Goliath. Our faith is in the Lord. He has placed me among this great army for a special purpose. I survived a terrible death to make me ready for what comes next.

December 21, 1835. We are very fortunate to have so many new brothers. It is strange not to speak Cherokee so much. Some are from many different places. Some are Mexican Tejanos who hate Santa Anna for stealing their sons, crops, and their way of life, for Mexico's own army. Germans, French, English, and a few members of some Red River tribes are among our ranks. We have all come to an understanding of each other just as we did when I first came to the Cherokees. I felt that we are part of a bigger tribe, like the Cherokee Warrior Society. Scouting for the Texican army was the right idea, after all. "Santa Annie" will have to watch out for us in the future. We hope to keep him awake at night like he has done for us. That makes for an even trade to me.

December 25. We go to celebrate Christmas with all of us from different places. A German man brought in a fresh cut evergreen. We decorated it with strings of popped corn, cut pieces of paper, and tin from a can to make a star. A few people knew Christmas songs. One could play the left-handed banjo, another plays a fife, and a harmonica. They have a good play. They got comfortable trying to keep everybody playing together. We have a nice time, but it is lonesome to not see my wife. We took time earlier to read the Bible in the book of Luke about the birth of Jesus.

We are enjoying the words, when several wagons have come up. General Houston has sent for our loved ones that could come! Ke-Ke and Say-te-Qua never looked so good to us! They are a welcome sight as the best Christmas present. The music flared up into some reels and some serious dancing. We did our best to stomp some dirt clods and not the women's feet. Say-te-Qua called our dance the "grasshopper stomp". The Tejano women have spent some time to dress her in a pretty new dress with a yellow rose in her hair. Say-te-Qua said that she wanted to surprise me by wearing a new dress for a special night together. She smelled so nice and she looked wonderful to me! She looked at me with those big brown eyes. All I could do was try to not step on her feet while we danced. She smiled sweetly as she made her way to dance with me. I was just beside myself. I have missed her so much! That is why I am here learning to be a decent soldier. I got all tongue tied like I did when I first met her. She was gracious, and wonderful. My love for her has grown stronger since we have been apart. It was well worth the wait to see her.

We danced. I managed not to trip over my feet. Say-te-Qua did a special dance called the "Shaw Dance" that was so wonderful. It made me so proud of her.

All soldiers gather for our first merit stripe on their
sleeve for good conduct. We are given two day's leave from
soldiering. We are told to stay within ten miles of camp. Just
in case of trouble there will be cannon fire to bring us running.
We are free to visit and catch up on our life. Say-te-Qua says
that I look good, but I need to be home soon so she can feed
me better. I miss her good cooking and the company of the
cook. We finally get to be alone to talk. These two days will
go by fast, but we will make the most of it.

The teamsters have come to take our family back home.
It was hard to see them go. I acted brave and tried to smile
so it would not make things any worse. Our commanding
officer came to tell us of some new assignments. We are told
of plans to build a new fort along the Trinity. The new fort
will help to control the flow of people going up and down
the Trinity, north and south. Commander Goyens told us
the East Fork is the mostly used by the Cherokee and Caddo
trade routes. They travel on canoes dug out of big cottonwood
trees. These water routes might be our only way to get goods
in a hurry as Mexico tries to block our supplies into Texas on
the Gulf of Mexico. We will have our family secure in a fort
soon. We are to be a sizeable force to deal with. Alone we
are nothing. Together we are a force that gets stronger by the
day. This time our fight does not leave us lacking some good
soldiers for battle.

January 5, 1836. We have some men returning from San Antonio. They tell us some details of the past week. The commander of the Mexican forces at San Antonio is Colonel Domingo de Ugratechea. He sent a detachment of 100 men to get their defensive cannon away to try to use it against them. The Texican forces came up in the fog. They crossed the river and surprised the Mexican soldiers. Texicans over took them, their guns, powder, and 100 pounds of lead shot. That is enough gun powder to make much good use of. All these goods have just been brought to us as most were captured from the Mexicans a month ago. We study tactics and how to act when the heat is on. We learn to think quickly and to follow orders. In the Cherokee camp many decisions are talked about among the warriors. In this army things are to be done and done quickly. The days are long and full of carrying out orders and doing many tasks. We are becoming more of a tribe since we depend so much on each other.

January 7. Our commander, William Goyens takes a look at the troops. He said, "Colonel Stephen F. Austin has been holding off the Mexican troops. He is to keep them boxed in for a month. He needs fresh troops to relieve some of the 300 men there. Our General George Collingsworth has been keeping General Cos from bringing in more supplies and troops through the port of Copano. Some men will go to Goliad; some are to go to San Antonio. The port of Copano is secured, but Commander Collingsworth will need more reinforcements at month's end. We will be sent there for a period of a month. The assignments are spelled out in the duty roster. We still need many more men to help hold the land for the Texicans. We are here like an ant trying to pull a mule uphill! The odds are full against us but we are stubborn towards anyone who would harm us. Back in Louisiana we were outnumbered by the smugglers. This time we are still against great odds, but these odds are much better than those we had before!

The Grass Fight at Goliad

Red Bird and I are to go to Goliad to bring supplies and more men to help give the other soldiers relief. Some soldiers have told us of Colonel Austin's attack on a pack train going to General Cos. They thought that the mules are carrying silver to pay the Mexican soldiers. The Mexicans are only carrying hay to feed their horses. They are due help themselves. We keep their forces in check by keeping their horses from being fed. They called this the "Grass Fight." Some of the Mexicans run to break out of our blockade. They do not go even a mile before they are captured. One is wounded. We are only shot at. It isn't the first time and it won't be the last, so only our pride is hurt. The Mexicans have been here. They were held at bay for over two months. We heard that they have killed many of their horses to slaughter for food to save on what little hay there is. It is foggy like it was a while back. We cannot see half a mile away. Trouble hides in low hanging clouds as we pray to be safe.

We fear that some of Cos's men may break away in the dark. We watch for lanterns, spooked deer, or any signs of movement. We hear a lot of foolishness about the goings on. We take four hour watches, rather than six hours. Commander Goyens says, "There is better service by taking shorter watches, for fatigue will make any person make bad mistakes." Lots of mistakes have been made here. They will make even more mistakes because they are ragged and tired out. We will stay sharp and ready. We took a lasso of rope and put it across the river. We tied it low on a tree close to the water line. If anyone comes by then we will keep them from passing by pulling the rope tight. We hear a boat coming close. We hold our breath to wait to fire on them. It is General Houston and some of his close aids. They are a welcome sight. We feared them to be the Mexican army. We have Mexican allies called Tejanos who hate what Santa Anna and Cos are doing here as much as we do. We did not like the idea of having to shoot someone. I do not know how it will be when that happens. We made General Sam welcome by pouring him some stout coffee. He sat still for a moment to take off his boots. He said it felt good to finally be at camp. He seemed positive and he looked like a chief in his leather jacket given to him by the Creeks. A good leader stands out from the rest. General Houston is a whole head taller than the rest of the men. The tribes respect him as friend that would not make war on them. That makes him a very big man. Big for being six feet and six inches tall! Just like King Saul in David's time. We are General Sam's own mighty men. Our company will come under the command of William Burleson who takes over Colonel Austin's troops. He is good as our commander Goyens, but he does not like us very much. We may look different but our heart is just the same.

Colonel Austin is going to the Northern Federal States to get some help in the form of loans and bonds. Commander Burleson takes the reins of power and gives us a good work over. We have never shoveled so many horse muffins in my life! We shovel all the stalls out. There is a whole large load of hay coming in that we have to stack up, like shoveling was not enough to do. This new commander is going to kill us if he does not let up some. He is only hurting himself more than us. Still it is no sweat off him to hurt us and our will to live. We got into bed and he called us out to do more chores!

A letter came from Say-te-Qua. She has learned to write with the help of some of the ladies of the Soldiers'

Society. This started to help the ladies not to suffer while all the soldiers are gone. The wife says that she wants to leave Fort Houston to go back to her tribe so she can be with Ke-Ke. I think right now that even Ke-Ke would be a welcome sight! She says that she has a big surprise for me when I get back home. It sounds like a good surprise for a change.

Governor Smith is removed from office

January 21, 1836. We are sent to Waterloo to make sure some delegates get about safely. There are some Federal Mexicans that say that they do not support Santa Anna after his attack on Zacatecas. Lorenzo DeZavala headed our group so he tried to keep tight reigns on things. Time was short so we rode hard to get there because we feared being captured by Mexicans that did not want them to join with our forces. We also feared that someone might shoot us all trying to get the bounty put on the Yucatan Rebels that General Santa Anna offered recently. Lorenzo DeZavala helped broker the arrangement for the Rebels' safe passage to come here. DeZavala has sent us with a messenger to take to Governor Henry Smith. They talk of working together with Governor Smith to stop Santa Anna. Having the Yucatan Rebels on our side would be a great partnership because they are angry against Mexico like the Tejanos! We arrive at the house where the governor is staying. Some Texican soldiers stopped us because we are dressed in plain clothes so we could travel without drawing attention to ourselves. Commander DeZavala takes the rifle away from one man as he grabs the other by the ear to push him against the house. This gives us the chance to get the upper hand just to get safely inside the house. He is eating a big bowl of stew. He is angry because we are interrupting his meal. These men want to become our allies and he is concerned over his soup becoming cold! We are now turned away inside the house by some soldiers in charge if guarding the governor. We pushed past them because we out rank them. We grabbed them to take away their weapons. We brought ourselves back into the room and bar the door. We tell the governor the purpose of our visit. The governor refuses their help because he calls us a traitor along with them. He asks us to leave, so we do. He is so immature and foolish! I went outside with the Yucatan delegates. They have some unkind words to say that are needed under the times we live. We go out to the horses to get a canteen of water. Red Bird has those soldiers that troubled us all tied up! I knew that they stopped beating on the door after a while. It is always the quiet people that you have to watch out for! The delegates told us that this was the third time they have come here to try to make a truce with us. This is the first time they made it inside the house to talk with Governor Smith. It was sad that a chance for peace slipped by us over someone who is not serious enough to be governor.

Lorenzo DeZavala opened the door to tell the governor that he is to come to come to review the troops by tomorrow morning. Governor Smith threw the bowl and broke it against the wall. DeZavala moved out of the way. He told him that we would feed him some breakfast if he came early enough for the troop review. The delegates said that this was the last chance for our alliance, so they are leaving tonight under the dark of the new moon. We are not happy about this either, so we take the rebels back to a fishing boat that brought them here safely. We watched the boat sail away along with our chance for a quick cure for our ills with Santa Anna and Cos.

Governor Smith is now visiting to give the troops a review. He did not show up here yesterday, so a detachment of men went to get him! He is at odds with the Consultation, the new representatives of the settlements. They feel that by dividing Santa Anna's forces may be a way to defeat him. The Governor says that he will not support any alliance with the Mexican Federals. He states that Texas is independent of Mexico, and all the high tariffs that we have to pay are wrong. We fear that his declaration against the Yucatan Rebels will cause good allies to turn against us. This is a terrible waste of good allies!

The Consultation sent a new representative to meet with Governor Smith urging him to be allies with the Mexican Federals, who still want order to come back to their land. Another Yucatan messenger has sent word for them to make it known of their sincere intentions. The Consultation representative said that the vote was taken by anticipating the Governor's refusal of their help. Governor Smith is to be removed from office in two days. His soldiers and guards are removed from his charge. Henry Smith is surprised at the Consultation's decision. He should not be, for they have warned him twice of what would happen if he refused help. They have done as they said. There is much confusion with the choices made by the governor, so there needs to be a settlement of the debate. An alliance would help keep us from using so many of our soldiers, and our weapons that we are short of. That must have been some good soup. I hope it was worth it. A full belly does not make for much peace of mind, for very long. There is a bigger need to see things better.

We continue our drills, and practice putting up the tents, and moving to a different camp. We have been practicing with the new rifles that have come in. They are new long rifles. They have good range, and the sights are reasonable. This new brass shell is better than pouring powder and lead shot, which tends to get wet in a hurry. Our practice gets us out in the rain. This new shell ammunition is different, but better. The barrel of the gun is less likely to get curled around your face from loading the patch and powder wrong. Some are old rifles salvaged from the 1812 War that were captured from the English. These are what I know how to use well. We have a practice with both weapons as we never know what we may have in front of us at time of battle. We know the Mexicans use both kinds as they take weapons as they capture goods for their use as they move along like grasshoppers in a wheat field.

General Burleson has us pulled back to Gonzales. He has us set up our camp over a week back. He still runs us ragged because he is angry over the provisional governor's lack of leadership. He had us move a rock wall from one side of the camp to the other side. We moved our camp twice since the month began. I keep thinking that he will leave here soon to go south. The soldiers that fought with Ben Milam at San Antonio told us about the battle of how General Cos held up in the Alamo mission. They fought a house to house battle in San Antonio. Commander Ben Milam was lost to a sniper's bullet the very first day of fighting. They celebrated the victory over General Cos against the terrible loss of many of their men. The Tejanos say that they wish to be rid of General Cos. They sent him home with a broken spirit and his tail between his legs. They all say that Texas can no longer be a part of Chihuahua or any other Mexican state. Many Tejanos in the ranks of the army that feel the same way since many have lost sons, farms, and all they own to the Mexican army. General Cos' men are now numbering 1,200. The new reports brought to us by the Tejanos report them numbering over 102 wounded, 125 dead. It took a day to count and recount the totals to get the numbers right. We read the report to General Sam as he is busy writing some of our own reports.

Their wounded are now healed up, and sent packing back to Mexico like the other 1,000 soldiers were. Their uniforms are taken from them and burned. Our commander is sending them back home in shame by wearing their red flannel underclothes. Their guns and cannons are now ours! They have French markings on them so we know where they came from. They are from the same place as our own weapons! The Mexican army will be ashamed of their loss to us! The Tejanos celebrate their loss as it means that we are closer to victory here in Texas. We pray for wisdom and to not to be too bold: as pride comes before the fall. Santa Anna will want revenge against San Antonio and the Tejanos. We wished we had the Yucatan rebels as allies as we are about to see the start of fighting a hornet's nest. We needed their help and now they might turn against us.

Who is the chief of the Texans?

A large group of Texican volunteers has been gathered there under Frances Johnson. He is a new and unproven commander. They did not recognize General Houston as the supreme commander here. They pushed him away from his visit to San Antonio. He was most angry as I did not blame him. He has been named the official head of the Texican army. None can say that he is not the commander, or anything less. So now these new men under his command won't listen. He pulled out a new Colt pistol and he fired up in the air three times. He makes them do right and obey his commands. There will be many people on all night guard duty and kitchen patrol. General Sam talked louder than I have ever heard him speak. His face was red as the setting sun. He gets strict with them and put them through their movements. He usually speaks like a friend and a father. Like any good chief worth his salt he was ready to back it up when he spoke! General Sam said that when he served under the command of Andrew Jackson, that many victories were lost in 1812 battles against the English. Federal soldiers refused to listen to simple orders that made room for the English soldiers to win many battles. These people are cut from the same cloth: more dangerous to us than Santa Anna and Cos put together. The lack of order and respect just puts us all in peril. I miss my wife and I wish we were all back in east Texas. I miss the Cherokee and our days catching horses.

Those were the better days for us. Our wives are back now in the Piney Woods where we wished we could be.

Tonight we read First Peter, Chapter 18, "Precious."

Governor Smith is forced from his office

General Houston said that the temporary Governor Smith is ordered to be removed by the Consultation of delegates. These delegates have ordered us to go quickly to Matamoros about a month ago. General Sam said that our army is so unorganized, under armed, and not manned very well. It would be a disaster to split up our army to go under the commander of Frances Johnson. General Houston said, "I make all the decisions here!" He is responsible for this army doing better. To divide us up to fight on two fronts would be a bad military move. We would be chopping off our own nose for no good cause!

February 1, 1836. The Consultation of delegates agreed to meet in early March at Washington-on-the Brazos. David Burnet is voted to be the provisional president. Governor Henry Smith had said that our meeting here would only alarm the Mexican government against us. I remembered that much. We made a report for General Houston. General Houston said, "We can't make friends with a mad dog!" We will build up our army, make ourselves strong, and take orders from no one! The conflict of "Who is in Charge?" has been debated. Some men have served under Frances Johnson, and some under James Fannin. Both are able commanders, but Lieutenant Governor James Robinson picks General Houston as the supreme commander. He has ruled that General Houston was wise by keeping our forces intact. It is truly unwise to split the army into two fronts by sending our troops into Matamoros. That makes General Houston in charge. The first order of business is concerning the governor's actions and lack of authority. Governor Henry Smith is officially removed from office. He no longer has any say in the matter. We went with a detachment of soldiers. We have now come in to ask the governor pack and be gone by tomorrow. He is not such a bad person, other than being stubborn and thick in the head. He just misses the point of having the Yucatan rebels to help us fight Santa Anna like the Tejanos do. We need all the help we can get since beggars can't be choosers. They are much needed help could not come quick enough. To turn away good allies is just unthinkable! He has some harsh words for us but we are used to harsh words from others since we came here. It wasn't the first time, and probably won't be the last time. The next morning we sent him packing for new quarters. He had another day, but he has worn out his welcome. He has to go as he is no friend to us. How did he ever become a governor? I continue to make reports for General Houston. I am one of the few of a dozen men who can read or write well enough to make a decent report to General Sam. We talked to each other to make sense of some of the details. General Houston laughed when we told him about the stew being so important to the governor. He shook his head and then he became angry over the loss of some possible new allies. We grew tired knowing that the new camp at Victoria was a far ride, so we asked permission to leave. General Sam asked us to stay here because we were all so tired from traveling so far, today. We slept on the ground and General Sam slept on a cot. He felt he could rest better with more people about him as guards acting for his safety. We woke early to go to Goliad. He asked us to go along because we all seem to get along so well. It felt good to be involved in being useful around here.

I woke earlier than anyone because I hurt from riding so far the past few days. I made coffee and some biscuits like Widow Lalaurie showed me. It was good to have some fresh bread to eat. General Sam likes that I try to be so helpful to him. General Houston left with us for Goliad to talk with Colonel Fannin and his men. He has not forgotten how they treated him when he called for all of them to muster together. Before this they ignored him, and he just rode off very angry. This time I would not want to be in their shoes: for General Houston is not someone that you would want to cross the wrong way. I am glad that we are on the same side. We go now to get things started early. We dress in plain clothes like we are horse wranglers. This is to test the colonel to see if his troops are ready for battle and watching out as he should. We arrived late, long after dark. Red Bird and I go in to scout him out. There is a man on guard duty asleep. Red Bird captures him. He ties him up well and gags him with a bandana to keep him from calling out. We look to see the other sentry asleep from drinking too much. He did not need to be tied because he was too far gone. We took his weapons and made sure he did not be a problem. We make the signal for General Sam to come in and he finds them all caught unaware. It seems that they should just hand over the "reigns of Texas to Santa Anna and Cos." This is what being so lazy will make possible. General Sam has quite a few unkind words for their commander and his troops. He put the man that was asleep on guard duty to in charge for a few weeks. He made the drunken man in charge of the kitchen chores for the next two months that follow. He could have been shot from what I understand. I would not want to be him or anyone in that company. We made all the proper reports that were requested. It was hard to see our commander so unhappy with the state of things here. We left him alone to ponder what to do next. He threw rocks across a river so we left him to his thoughts. He sat and smoked his pipe so we kept watch for his safety so he could consider his next plans.

Santa Anna attacks San Antonio

February 3, 1836. We hear that Santa Anna has crossed the Rio Grande River to take revenge for the earlier loss by General Cos. He would probably head for the new settlements first, but he does not. He wants to take back San Antonio since that has been what Cos has lost. General Johnson asks us to volunteer to go to San Antonio to head off the spread of Santa Anna's troops trying to retake San Antonio. General Houston sent his messenger to tell us to stay put, because that is Colonel Travis' detail. We have no choice but to obey our orders. General Sam ordered the Colonel Travis to destroy the Alamo mission in January. The Alamo could not be used for any good purpose other than giving Santa Anna a strong hold like General Cos has tried to do. It is the only defendable position on the river on this side of the San Antonio Road. It would be his stepping stone into Texas to give him a place of refuge. We have standing orders to write for General Sam because he is ill today from the burden of command. We helped him as I am one of the few who can read and write in our company. I am happy to help as General Sam is one of the few able commanders that truly make any sense around here. He thinks before he acts and he well considers what he does. We read the mail he gives us and we write notes on what they basically want to know or do. General Sam wanted us to do what we thought was best on the minor items and leave the more important details to him. He gave us a rise in rank and the freedom to travel between the camps to run errands, taking count of what supplies are needed. We kept him well informed. He asked about the morale of the troops in the different camps. They grumbled too much and many were wild as a bear let loose in a cabin.

We saw Captain Goyens. He was glad to see us. He had us send orders to General Sam of some news that some soldiers were coming from New Orleans called the "Greys". He also asked for what supplies we had a good quantity of would trade for what we needed to a different company. I had some ideas and shared them with him. It was nice to see a friendly face for a change, for many soldiers are not happy that their commander has to take orders from General Sam. Someone has to be the big boss, or "vato" to take the role of supreme commander of Texas. He is our new Texican war chief.

General Houston has sent a small detachment of men to San Antonio. James Bowie with about 30 men is commanded to hold off the Mexican troops. Bowie's men make a complement of soldiers to join up with Colonel Travis. We are to stay put here to make a front to keep the Mexican soldiers from attacking the settlements. A wooden fence is no stone wall, but it may be enough to slow down the enemy. If we leave here they will be prone to attack. We must stay here to help keep things running smooth. All the newcomers here are wild as a mustang. Our rank has been raised and so has our problems. How can we help make a soldier out of something so uncertain?

February 11, 1836. Commander Neill has to leave San Antonio due to Typhoid fever claiming his wife and child. That was just terrible to hear. General Houston said that this James Bowie would have to carry the burden of command. We talk. Rather he talks, and I listen. He asks advice of me, for me to be plain spoken. I tell him that I feel that we will get more men trained to send to help. We will keep the Mexican army from being able to get to the new settlements. He listens well to makes good notes. Frequently he asks for opinions to consider the different points of view. I am not a good judge of things, but I have seen so much that needs to be done for us to make some progress here. Maybe what I know is worth a few jujus, after all. I write things down so I won't forget. Our lives have been so busy that many things are worth remembering with all the reports we have to write to our commanders and General Sam. We teach other men to write so they can write letters and read the Bible.

The Attack on the Alamo
February 26, 1836. Santa Anna's army has arrived in San Antonio less than a week ago. He crossed over the Rio Grande

with a strong mission to take back San Antonio for the revenge of the capture General Cos a year ago. A messenger has arrived for General Houston. She is the spy that reports that the Mexican forces have over run the city! Colonel Travis and a group of about 100 men with some Mexican farmers have held-up in the Alamo mission. James Bowie fell under the Typhoid fever. Colonel Travis is now their commander. It was the stepping stone into Texas we fear. What can be done to secure that place as it is the place that General Cos was defeated. Santa Anna would be looking for a bloody revenge, for fear always brings death with it. Revenge brings no satisfaction, as death only brings more of the same.

Rosa Lee, the Texican spy

We have learned more about the young woman called Rosa Lee. She rode two different horses to death to get here. The report is the terrible news that the Alamo has been overrun by thousands of Mexican troops! She said that over 500 Mexican soldiers are dead, or wounded. All of the Texicans are killed! She is terribly shaken and weak where she has to be helped. She passed out and fell still to the ground. It made me sad because it reminded me of Delephine. We have Red Bird tend to her since we have no doctors here. She does not want help but she is so tired that she needs some help. He has her drink some mesquite tea and rest several hours to give her a chance to feel better so she can think.

She is the Texican spy we heard word of. She listens for news of Mexican troop movements to let us know of future plans and battle plans. She seemed sad and tired from the stress of a month or so.

She wakes up wanting water and bread. She eats a few bites and she starts talking about the Mexicans raising the red flags all through their camps. They played the Song of the Dead. She called it "the Deguello". She says that this means that the Texicans are to be shown no mercy in battle. They aren't to take any new prisoners. General Houston said that she is to stay here for a week to rest. I am to write notes since I am one of her guards to protect her while she visits here. We ask her not to speak any more until she feels stronger. Red Bird gives her something strong to drink to make her sleep for the rest of the night. She is ragged for being pushed so hard to travel so far. We set a dependable guard outside to watch for her safety. General Houston asked all his aids to meet with him. He is making the plans to stop the Mexican army in their tracks. We fear more towns being under their influence, making it more difficult to protect ourselves. The men in our ranks are so green that they are like new persimmons. They want to fight but they aren't ready for battle against seasoned and better trained soldiers. We have been part of the big push to make plans to stop the Mexican army at all costs. She said that her own family is in jeopardy, so doing nothing means that it is a matter of time before the fight comes to where we live. We all have a role to play, so we are all risking our lives and all we have if need be. Something worth having requires some sacrifice.

The New Texas Constitution

March 1, 1836. We rode with General Sam so that he would be more secure. Delegates arrive to go to Washington-on-the-Brazos. We ride together so we can make good use of the traveling time. Five other delegates rode with us, and they discussed some of their concerns. The scouts rode "point" ahead of us so that can see if trouble is coming. We will have to go to war. The delegates spoke of their concerns. General Houston wrote pages of notes and questions. He brought some old maps of the land grants, and rolled them out and they looked at them while we let the horses rest and graze on the tall grass. We laid the map out flat on a big tree stump. They laid stones out to represent the placement of our troops. Commander Goyens took small pieces of wood to show the towns where the Mexican troops are moving. We need more "rocks" in our favor, and less "wood" to do any good. This was a fine way to see the details of things better. We have a lot riding on this meeting. We have our work cut out for us because there is a great need for more Texican troops.

The weather has turned nasty, and cold. We broke out heavy gear. It felt more comfortable. We finally reach the building: a long dog trot house made of sawmill lumber brought from Jefferson. There is not a fireplace, or a wood-burning, cast iron stove to keep it warm! While this was built it was unusually fair, and warm for the season, but not for today. The room is full of delegates from the different settlements. They are talking of drawing up a paper that declares them to be no longer the rule of Mexico, and that we no longer have to pay them high tariffs on our goods. The lack of a fire made all the delegates work like bees. There was much debate and some only wore out their welcome.

The oil lantern made the only heat beside the crowd of many people. The wind blew, and the house rattled like a barrel. Everything stopped until the lantern is lit again. Some have been here for several weeks getting things ready. It is well worth it. Collin Mack Kinney wrote out a good part of the document. He argued some with General Sam about some details on our break with Mexican rule. Many have petty issues that just conflict with the older land owners and earlier Mexican land grants being made null and void. This was more about opening up a big can of worms! One man wanted to allow slavery when we become independent! This is not independence by any means. It was not a petty issue to raise here. Neither was the notion to move the Cherokee out of the piney woods of east Texas. Other Red River tribes are mentioned, also. Red Bird kept quiet, but he was very angry. He wasn't alone, because arguments broke out. The unity we hoped for fell apart for the rest of the night. We took a few men out in the cold to calm their short tempers.

General Sam had some harsh words, but then he had regret over what was said. We broke the meeting for the night because the tired souls had little rest and less reason left in them. Some men went out into the cold to resolve their issues. We need to save our strength to fight the Mexican army, not each other! General Sam was angry and put-out that people were so unreasonable. He went out in the cold to walk for over an hour. People slept on the floor and some delegates stayed in some tents that were put up earlier. The fear is that if we stay here too long that Santa Anna could send his troops in to capture us all.

March 2, 1836. The delegates talk about the final draft of their constitution. The Alamo attack has lasted over two weeks. The cannon fire can be heard ten miles away, a delegate said. We keep watch as they all work more to finish this draft of their paper. They are encouraged to come to an agreement soon so something can be done. The sooner they all sign, the better for us all. The debate goes back and forth on issues on the Mexican conflict. Two delegates said that we should petition Mexico to take us back into their fold. Most delegates stared at them like they are crazy. "We are past the point of no return. Coming back to them now would be a sign of weakness. We cannot allow them to take revenge on us, just for protecting ourselves!" General Houston said that and more. Collin Mack Kinney argued that the longer the delegates waited, the better the chance our meeting place might be captured. That settled all the debate. They all know that to delay is to make the problem worse. The cold weather makes for trouble for some are complaining of being uncomfortable, and cold. The General Sam said, "We need to sign to complete our task, and our sworn duty." Being cold is better than being at the point of a bayonet, or saber. They sign at almost eleven, at night. About midnight, we passed out some strong drink in the form of some 'corn squeezings'. These are offered out to those who wanted to partake. It is to celebrate the new Texas constitution. An election for the new president of Texas is soon to follow. The other occasion today is General Houston is 40. He said that he has been so busy that he had forgotten what day it is. He raised a glass to drink a toast: "to Texas!" We will stay a few more days unless we are attacked by the Mexican army. Others are offering another toast: "to General Sam!" Many soldiers here have much to lose as some have lost everything to Mexico. They have attacked some of the delegates' families by taking their sons as prisoners, to fill the Mexican army's ranks. Many have lost their stock, and their crops. We are all next if we aren't careful. This all seemed all too familiar to me.

Today, we read Joshua Chapter 4, Verses 13-19. "12 Stones"

The Retreat from Gonzales

March 08, 1836. General Houston ordered Commander Fannin to retreat with 374 soldiers who are badly trained, and ill equipped to command. The news of the new attack on the Alamo has been told to us. Gonzales is becoming too much of a chore to hold with the few soldiers that we have. We took a zigzag course going from La Grange to San Felipe. We hope that Mexican soldiers looking for fresh horses and food do not over take us on the road. At San Felipe we hear the terrible news of the battle at Goliad. Many soldiers are taken prisoner. The messenger escaped by covering himself with blood and playing dead. He said there was no time to count the many dead or wounded. There was more information coming the next few days. We now have the stress and the burden of another attack where we are to hold our ground to protect where we are. David had Goliath, and General Houston has Santa Anna and Cos.

The Texas navy has not been able to keep the Mexican army from getting supplies, and reinforcements. They have the small advantage for now. That will not always be so. We must pray for the wisdom to do what is right in the sight of the Lord. Santa Anna seeks to break our spirits and our revolt against him! The days all wash together. We are so busy with so little rest.

The Cherokee Treaty is ignored by the Senate

March 9, 1836. The treaty signed by Cherokee Chiefs Bowles and Mush is a month old. John Forbes, John Cameron, and William Goyens asked the Cherokee to stay peaceful in case of war with Mexico. The Cherokee have no plans to do otherwise. The Texicans want a written promise of our continued alliance. They wish to stay on good terms with the Cherokees. This land belongs to the Cherokee. Chief Bowles and Mush were gracious to let others have some land from which to live and trade from. We are their guests. Chief Bowles asks, "Why do we have to make treaties on land that we fought for with our own blood? I am the peace chief, not the war chief! We have managed to live here and prosper trading horses, salt, and lead shot. We hunt for deer and buffalo to trade their hides with the French in Louisiana. Texas is our hunting ground that we share with you and all the tribes. We are different but we have to learn to trust each other. Our vision for the land is different than theirs."

It seems they came to Texas to find a place of their own since they were pushed out of Kentucky and the Carolinas. This is the Cherokee's last refuge, to live in east Texas. Santa Anna broke the treaty that was set with President Maximilian to make good trade. The chief then hands the "talking stick" to the next person to speak in council. John Cameron said that we could plant fields of corn annually, and grow winter wheat, and oats and sell, or barter for things that we need. This will keep us able to feed ourselves." We are independent persons. Mister Cameron then hands the fancy stick to Mister Goyens. He says that he will dedicate two teams of oxen, and three mules for pack animals. He said that he has a good harrow and two plows to donate. He and two of his sons have offered to help the Cherokee grow a large amount of crops like squash, corn, beans, garlics, and onions. People who farm have little time for trouble, or those who seek to make any trouble.

Commander Goyens takes the 'talking stick' so he can speak. He said, "The Texas Senate has refused to see the need for a peace treaty since the Texicans aren't at war with the Cherokee in east Texas. The Cherokee wanted this as a pledge of their support of the Texicans as their new government begins. They are a peaceful people as warfare carries too high a price.

The Cherokee will fare well in spite the denial of Chief Bowles' treaty. We will let farming help supplement our needs when hunting is poor. We will still trade horses for barter between us." Mister Goyens then handed the talking stick to Mister Forbes. He encouraged the young men to participate in the ballgames, like the Cherokee tradition states. Lacrosse is played to teach them to work together, to make their senses keen to keep them strong. We should encourage them to play games to show off their skills. This will boost their morale and offer some good prizes: one of them is a new deck of cards, two pairs of bone dice, some seed corn, a new iron knife, and forty mustangs in the corral. A new horse is always a good way to soothe any bad tempers.

"Tradition says that the ballgames must be played to dedicate the first planting that we have, and if the war chief feels that battle is coming," the Cherokee elders said. The field will be cleared by burning off the tall grass. In two days it is cleared of all debris. The young men go through a ritual of the sweat lodge, and then fasting for half a day. Then they feast for half a day. When it is light, the games begin. The warriors line up to play the game. They carry a long stick that has a rawhide net at one end. The opposing sides are painted up after drawing lots to see who in red, and who is painted black bands on their chest, arms and back. The game is played at a furious pace. They cover over a mile running to the goals marked by a red cloth banner tied to a tree, at one end, the black cloth banner at the other end. They run and hit the rawhide ball keeping it toward their goal. They both play after some near mishaps with their sticks being used too rough. The game ends at sundown. The red team wins according to the number of stones piled on their side of the goal tally. We feel that the Cherokee are willing to stay allies even without a treaty.

CHAPTER SIX

The Alamo, Runaway Scrape, and the Road to San Jacinto

Friday, March 13, 1836. The word arrived of the attack on Commander Travis. He is held up in the Alamo like Cos did a year ago. People are leaving by the droves, clogging up all the roads leading to Natchitoches Louisiana, along the San Antonio Road. Santa Anna is personally chasing the members of the Texas government to capture, and kill anyone associated with them. The Mexican forces are going from San Antonio, to San Felipe to catch up with the Texas government officials. They will be wise to stay free of trouble. It seems that trouble seems to find us no matter what we do, or where we live. The Alamo should have been destroyed after General Cos was pushed out of there last year. His defeat just proved that it is not a place easy to defend with any amount of troops. We just prayed for those at San Antonio because no amount of men could defend that place for long, against such odds.

The Run Away Scrape

We are called to assembly. Our orders are to go to the river crossing at the Sabine. We have to travel with new and old settlers to protect them from Mexican raids or to keep the peace from failing each other. As we camped there was bad blood between old and new. This made it hard to have a few hours of peace to rest. Some of the groups are divided up to make a different route to get there. These wagons are lined up in a row. There was a fork that meandered a bit to the east. The more troublesome are sent along the right fork of the road. Our orders were changed for our troop to be in charge of these wonderful people. Red Bird tried to keep me from losing my temper, because orders are orders. A majority of the population is heading north, and east. It has poured down a steady rain which has made some wagons stuck in the mud. These wagons are overloaded with too many goods that are not really necessary. Some goods were pulled out and left for the return trip if they can make it back soon.

Commander Goyens joined with us today to get a report of how the days of travel have gone. He was not too happy with report of the whole detail. It is a bad mess of things. The trip has been failing to get these people to Shreveport in a short time. I did not know if it was any safer there from what I remember. It was always good to go to trade days, but now it is the last place I want to see. There are too many memories of my days with Delephine to come here. These people have not sacrificed all they have like I have done. They are selfish and foolish to have so much that they don't really need.

We rode five days to get there. It would normally take three days of riding hard, but under these rules we have to go much slower to be safe so no one falls behind. As we come to each town more people are added to our care. It seems the roads on a fair day's count not meet this demand. Thousands have left their homesteads trying to cross the flooded rivers, from the rain of the past night. It just poured down, like the bottom dropped out of the bucket. We are at Groce's Raft Ferry is running all day, with people pushing to get ahead of others that have been patiently waiting for their turn to cross. We are here to keep order, and to protect the settlers from the Mexicans, and each other. A man crossed in front of others to push ahead to the next groups to cross this hour. I tried to stop him but he used a copper pan on my temples. I finally grabbed it away from him, as this man is not right. Red Bird rode up on his pinto pony. He came to my aid to stop the man from moving ahead or running over me as he pushed in the front of the line. The man pulled out a knife and he tried to take a swipe at Red Bird several times. Red Bird took away his knife in a short time. I tried to see straight as my head was foggy for a piece. Commander Goyens rode up as he got word from one of the new scouts what has just happened. The new settler told our commander, "I am someone important in San Antonio! My wagon should have already been across! This mean Indian and this slave have tried to stop me!" Commander Goyens jumped down from his horse as he pulled that man down to the ground. He had some unkind things to say. Red Bird picked me up from the ground as our commander stood over that man. I told the commander what has happened about the man cut into the line with an overloaded wagon. Commander Goyens pushed back the canvas of the wagon. He started pulling goods out of it that were not really needed. He pulled out a bathtub, an iron bedstead, a dozen copper pots and pans. The settler argued that was his wife's bathtub and she needed her things. Commander Goyens pulled out his pistol and he shot four holes into it! He said, "Here is what you need! This will be you and all of us if Santa Anna has his way! This bathtub won't save you from his wrath! Red Bird, take this man to the very back of the line. We are in greater danger from each other, because if this loaded wagon turns over the raft, then it will take a whole day to replace the guide ropes to cross the Sabine again." Red Bird told him in Spanish, "Ah-ho!

Vamanos Al-feine!" "Yes, let's go to the end!" He meant it because he was tired and he looked to have some blood on him. Red Bird looked fierce. He did his part to keep the peace. Even a Cherokee healer has to be a fierce warrior sometimes. I was fine, only my pride was hurt more than my thick head with a knot added to it. I came back later to find others have picked up those copper pots. I wanted a few of them for trade with the Indians we meet. One of those pots has a dent from my thick head.

When it got too dark, the raft crossings have to be stopped for a while. In about an hour the full moon rose to give enough light to continue crossing. That moon was a pretty sight. The people waiting have their spirits lifted once they know that they will cross in the matter of an hour. We continued to load up the rafts until the early morning hours. I was given easier duty because my left forehead is swollen in size and it changed in color. My head was wrapped with a piece of linen to make it feel better. My hat did not fit so well for the time being. I rested but I kept my eyes open wide because it was a busy day. It was hard to rest even though I was so tired. In the east, Venus is rising on the horizon, as a morning star. I think of the beautiful sight of my wife, and how I did not plan to spend so much time away from her. I just wanted to protect her, and not lose her like my sweet Delephine. The crowd of people is more of a trickle. The ferryman asked to have the raft at least half full so that it does not turn over in the heavy river currents. They changed to new mules to keep things moving along. It is threatening rain again, probably from all the big storms east of us. We have not heard of more troop movements, or any more orders. The people waiting engaged in some bartering for what they needed. We have to be present to prevent any squabbles from breaking out. We ended up with some coffee, and some glass jars of peaches in sweet water. Some of the people are just grateful for our help to get them across as quickly, and safely as possible. The people waiting said that the days of paying high tariffs and ruining our trade is over. The "important man" at the end of the line finally got his chance to cross. He has nothing to say to us. My head beat like a drum so I was relieved of duty by Commander Goyens. I watched as Red Bird crossed his arms and he looked angry. After the ferry crossed we were all relieved for we do not have to cross the rough river on that raft. I have no argument with them. I just wished that people would quit using my head like it was a lacrosse ball!

Our company rode back to a camp that was safe on a hill. The younger soldiers are posted to guard things so we get to sleep past the early row call in the morning since we are placed on sick call. I did not know that Red Bird has been cut on the arm by that stupid man! He had it bundled up good and he would not let on to make things any worse. He checked on the knot on my head. I felt bad because my brother was hurt worse than I knew. It is always some foolishness or greed that causes people harm. All this trouble over a bathtub, some copper pots, and an arrogant fool! The bad thing is that we are under the burden of a tyrant that has no regard for anyone. That makes normal people lose their sense of reason. I think I am losing my mind and my abundant patience.

March 12. A few more days have passed. My head still ached badly so I have my duty reading reports that come into our camp. This has been difficult for long. The Mexicans have over stepped their authority by attacking Zantacas, and now San Antonio! We cannot allow them to rein over us and attack us here. This army is able, and willing to protect our home, no matter what the odds against us. The last of the settlers came early this morning. They are about to cross. A few people show up at the last moment. It is decided that we should now cross the river into safety. We crossed but the whole time fear struck me about going back into Louisiana. It was my home for most of my life. Now I feel like a stranger here in what was my home in Louisiana. I threw up during the raft crossing. It made me sad to think about the last time I was on this side of the Sabine. I was relieved of duty for I was under the weather.

A week has passed. We are ordered to cross back over to the Texas side because of the arrival of more people to cross. This has been a very busy week full of scared and confused people. I have counted over 350 wagons, not counting the goods lined up on the shore. It looked like trade day was being held here! Many horses are tried into a large remuda. We are to bring these back to our camp outside Jefferson. These are needed at Groce's plantation to outfit the new soldiers. It is a time of war so we must do as we are ordered. I thought about that silly man that brought a bathtub, and his dozen copper pots. It was frightful the things the people think that they need. God gives us all we need and then some. The most important was some common sense. The main thing that we need is some rest. It will be another day before our watch here is over. We tried to eat some chicken soup and some hot coffee. Good food helped keep me strong, for the watch is over at midnight. I pray daily for wisdom on what to do here with this army.

We will stay here at Jefferson for the time being. Some goods come into Jefferson. We ordered a detail to load the goods after we checked over the list. Half the guns listed are lost and the loads do not match up! At least with the older rifles the lead shot and powder are not hard to match up. A few kegs of powder are wet so we had to write that on the manifest. Some things are missing all together. We have to try to justify this to the order manifest.

A messenger from General Houston sent orders and appreciation to us for the Sabine crossing going well under the stress of waiting, and trying to keep things orderly. General Sam said that we would be gathering more men to help us once the news of the slaughter at San Antonio of the Texicans. The place of the meeting and training is secret at this time. The great fear is that the Mexican army will be taking more towns, and taking more innocent lives. We had a short prayer meeting to settle some nerves. It was the best thing to do as some time was need to sort things out and show some respect to God who has been so merciful to all us to prosper in this difficult time. Red Bird spoke in Spanish and French to make all the words know. He spoke very well for someone who is not a Christian. I think maybe he has been a Catholic because of the missionaries he knew as a youth before he came to Texas. We prayed for all our enemies to give up this terrible fight so we can go back home. Often we are so busy with duties that we can't gather together as we should to worship God and show our unity as brothers. We can't forget what is important as we can't have a society that forgets God, or to be civilized to each other. This is what we read for today:

Acts Chapter 9, "Persecution, and Pressure."

Hiding in plain sight

March 17, 1836. The messenger of General Houston came with orders to go to the other side of the river to Jared Groce's plantation, a mile from the crossing. I remember riding past here with Delephine when we first crossed into Texas. This time I feel more welcome as this will be our new place to train. We are outside the camp waiting for the new recruits to arrive. They trickle in in groups of twenty or so. Some of them are loners that are wild as any mustang. Others are green as a new persimmon! I helped send the new men to find the camp. All the while looking for those who might be spies trying to undo our effort to train the men. There are many men coming since the word has got out about the attacks on the Texicans, and the offer of a land bonus to those that are willing to be loyal, and fight. Red Bird and I pushed twenty horses with the help of some Tejano wranglers into a newly made corral. These fresh horses will be put to some good use in battle. Soon, we hope. We have some recent letters from our wives. Red Bird read to me what my wife said in Cherokee. She is sad because I am gone too long. Ke-Ke would be a welcome sight right now. Our lack of sleep and lack of dedicated men will cost us in the long run if things do not turn around soon.

March 18, 1836. General Houston arrives with his close aids. He arrives on the far side of the camp wearing plain clothes, rather than his usual uniform. He asks to keep his identity a secret. He wants to say he appreciated how we helped clear our part of over 5000 people living between the Colorado, and Brazos Rivers. Juan Seguin is here with the general, who is also hiding his identity. They want to size up the men, and see what they are really like. The river has gone down and the men are able to cross the river without having too much trouble. It does not take three days to cross, as it did moving the settlers at the Runaway Scrape. The newspapers call it by this name so we named it the same way in our reports. We take stock of who is here wandering around. We send all the wandering men towards camp. General Sam and Juan Seguin are making their judgments of which men would make good scouts which are to be cavalry and infantry. Discipline is sadly lacking for too many of the men. Some are wild as any mustang. Some will be good soldiers, with a little work. Some need a great deal of work. Some I wonder how they found their way here.

General Sam has made his rounds among the men to get an idea of their attitude and skills. General Sam then stands next to Juan Seguin. The men realize who they have been talking to the past few hours. He asked them to stand together in several lines. He asks them to please listen, and save all questions, until after he finished speaking. The men all stood together. The General asked the men he picks to stand to one side. These are the men who will handle the remuda of horses and wagons. Commander Juan Seguin picks the men for the infantry: the troops that will do the ground fighting. The men are still a bit nervous that General Sam was walking around, being unknown to them. He is quickly sorting them all out. One older man is a good blacksmith. He will be able to teach at least one more man how to work iron. Another will be a farrier to tend to the horses. Others will learn to use cannons. It all goes well as things start to fall into place. There is no shortage of men to put on the night and evening watch. The kitchen patrol will be full for months to come. It is better them, than us! Guard duty will be full of the new-comers.

General Sam lowers the boom

A few hours have passed. General Sam now is dressed like a general. Those that showed contempt for him have been squared away to their new duties. The other soldiers are anxious to hear of their assignments. "The training that you are about to receive will help you do your tasks by being more efficient. You may not like it, at first, but you will learn to listen! Now is not the time for you to talk. Right now you will listen, and do as you are told! When you are assigned to do something, you had better do as asked." Some men still managed to talk out loud. General Houston keeps talking, without stopping to scold them, for interrupting. General Sam said, "The mass exodus of people in what the newspapers call the 'Run Away Scrape' has become why you are here to help stop the Mexican incursion far into east Texas. You will stop the Mexicans, even if it means to lay down your lives! You are promised some land if you are willing to fight for it: to earn it! The Officer of the Day, Commander Seguin will give you your orders. He is a Tejano who fights alongside us. When you are to practice doing your drills, many innocent lives hang in the balance. Some are as simple as marching in a straight line. Learn how to follow orders! Time is short and there is much to learn."

Commander Seguin took command. He spoke Spanish to Mexicans siding with the Texicans. There are many that are willing to fight. Commander Seguin takes them and gives them their assignments. Commander Seguin then speaks in English to explain, "Whatever task you are given, it is important that you do it to the best of your ability, even if it seems tedious, it is necessary. To not follow our instructions means trouble not for just you, but for all of us. We are in this together: our differences of whom we are, and where we come from does not matter. We must stop Santa Anna, or whoever is against us!" The men were rowdy when General Sam spoke. These same men kept talking when Commander Seguin gave his orders. General Sam came up and Commander Seguin stopped talking. General Sam then took the commander's duty roster, and walked up to the rowdy men. He pulled out a pistol and shot it right behind the men who are still being rebellious. Their ears must have rung terrible being so close to the gunshot. The men rubbed their ears and took stock of what was going on. Commander Goyens asked the men's names to find a spot for them on guard duty, and kitchen patrol. This made the men speechless for once. There was no more debate of who still is in charge.

Letters have come from Shreveport by some settlers wanting to return to their homesteads. A handful of us are able to read, or write. We are asked to read some of the letters. A report is made to General Sam about what some people are saying and wanting to know. A list of names and addresses are being made. A map is being marked to show their parish and towns. Our commander said that the settlers need to stay clear and out of the way for the time being. We do not need the mess we had at Groce's Crossing along the Louisiana border. People got bogged down in the mud by holding others up from making progress. We will not be guilty of being the "hold-up" of using our troops away from where they are needed. There was no debate, or comment from any of the men. Commander Goyens went to the ferry crossing to cut the ropes. He ordered the raft burned. The ferryman protested to no avail. His loss is our gain. This will keep those people out of our hair for a few weeks. We need the rest from all that worry for a while.

The news of the Alamo loss

March 12, 1836. The news came of the fall of the Alamo with the loss of all the Texicans! Commander Goyens reported it to the new men. General Houston hears the report of a Texican spy. He knew of the final attack of the Alamo that happened on February 26, by March 11. He has been quiet to not destroy the morale of the new men. He has more news of the battle going on at Goliad. "March tenth, I was in east Texas, looking for more volunteers to build up our army. A lot of people said that they would rather pay high taxes to General Cos, and Colonel Antonio Tenorio, the tax collector. General Sam said, "Those days are far past us. We cannot go back to their control, any more. We follow our cause because it is the right thing to do. Not out of fear, but out of necessity." This is our new anthem. It is too easy to give up hope.

March 29, 1836. The men have changed considerably these past two weeks. They are now more like soldiers than they were when they came. They are ready to fight, even though the members of the Texas government want the army to attack the Mexicans. General Houston says, "I am the Supreme Commander of the Army. I am the person in charge!" General

Houston made it clear: "you will listen when I say listen. You will speak when I ask a question. And you will fight when I say fight! These are my orders." General Houston then said, "I will be judged right for waiting to attack the Mexican army, when all is said and done." There was no open debate about the General Sam's orders, for no one wants extra guard duty, and kitchen patrol. We will wait until the time is right to do battle. When we do we will fight with all our might. Our patience is tried at times by some of the greenhorns who arrived here. We are ready to be back with our families. We are only ready for the fight to be over.

General Houston has been on the Brazos the previous week, looking at troop movements. He said, "The Mexicans camped so close to his hiding place that he could smell what they had for lunch. We waited for their siesta so we could leave before they posted the late afternoon guard." He also said, "The Mexicans are twenty miles up from San Felipe. They are in pursuit of the members of the Texas government. Members are being hunted down to be killed by them. They will keep a good distance, far away from their wrath.

April 1, 1836. General Sam asks several of us to have council with him. He has out on patrol the past two days. He has been writing and making notes on troop movements. I offered to help him write reports again. He needs some relief from the burden of command. He sits quietly sat and smoked his pipe. He finally speaks. He asks for us to be ready to help the new troops train and keep them in check. He tells us he wants to talk about some things. General Sam visits to talk about his early experiences with the Cherokee. These are some of his happier days. It was fun to think about something else for a while.

When he was about twenty years old he was new to the Cherokee tribe. He shared a tepee with four other young warriors. Since they disturbed the peace of the camp, they are on the end of the camp. He said early in the afternoon he sees a rattlesnake sunning on a rock. General Sam said that he caught the snake by pinning it to the ground with a long forked stick. He holds the snake behind the head and then wraps the snake's mouth with loops of sinew to keep the mouth shut. He then placed the snake in their bedrolls and then settled in like he was asleep, waiting for his brothers to discover it. He got tired of waiting so he went outside to get wood for the fire because it turned colder. The rattling noise starts so his Cherokee brothers tore down the dew cloths all the way around the teepee. They knocked over the teepee trying to get outside, away from the snake. The elders came and saw that the snake's mouth was tied shut. They held it up to show the others. It was good to see General Sam laugh for the first time in a long time. They had to sleep out in the cold because it had to be daylight to set up a teepee. We laughed and talked about more pleasant things that made us think of better days.

The News of the Slaughter at Goliad

April 2, 1836 George Childress is the lawyer that helped draft the Texas Constitution a month ago. Thomas Jefferson Rusk is now the Secretary of War. They came to our camp to encourage General Houston to attack the Mexicans army without delay. These men do not realize what a mistake to try to tell General Sam the where and when, to do anything. He is in charge. He has the reins over what we do, and when. He thanks them for their kind advice. He sends them to review the troops, and see the camp. General Sam has the Officer of the Day keep them busy. A Tejano scout showed them around. Then he has orders to send them on their way. Mister Rusk tells General Sam how the Mexicans have chased them for over a week from Harrisburg all the way to the Gulf coast. Some thought that they might end up past the Louisiana border like the Runaway Scrape. Shreveport would not be a safe place to hold up for a shelter.

Assembly is called. General Sam addresses the troops for their benefit. "I am the Commander. So the burden of when and where we take on battle is my decision. When it is all said, and done... I will be judged to be right for waiting.

Be patient for you will be told when the time is right. A week ago Santa Anna was trying to catch the members of the Texas government at Harrisburg, where the members were staying a few days earlier. They then headed to Lynchburg, at the junction of the San Jacinto River and Buffalo Bayou." General Sam continues his speech to the men telling them of how the Mexicans have closely followed the government representatives. Colonel Burnet pushed his men all the way to Galveston Bay. The Texans have set sail waving to the detachment of Mexicans on shore were cursing them." General Sam said, "This proves that our smaller forces can out run them. We can defeat them, if we are wise to use common sense against them. So their numbers are not what you are to think of. Rather see the defeat of their leader, Santa Anna. Then the rest of their force will crumble." If you cut the head off the snake then the rest of it curls up and dies. Some men talked out of turn. General Sam looked at the Officer of the Day, the one who makes the duty roster. The men then asked permission to speak. One man asked, "How many are in their army?" The general said, "Over 800 men form their ranks. Their number is very important, but our great advantage is our strategy, and the element of surprise. The Mexicans have camped on the small plain between the two streams of Buffalo Bayou, and San Jacinto." He continues and we take more notes. "Besides all this, there is the heinous loss at the Alamo, February twenty-sixth. There is more news that is bad. Trouble often comes in three waves. We have lost the men at Goliad that were taken prisoner! They were marched out and away from the Mexican camp. These brave men are shot like mad dogs!" The men shouted their disapproval. The visitors tremble from their outburst of anger. "We must do as we have planned to finish the new fort on the Trinity. We are going to our new camp on Buffalo Bayou, eight miles from the Mexican camp. The ferry at Lynchberg is under the Mexican army's control. These 800 Mexicans have settled into their camp on Buffalo Bayou, at San Jacinto. We will move to our new camp, soon. The Mexicans have given great chase to the Texicans. They are run ragged, and their forces are tired out. We now have 910 men to fight all these Mexicans. It is a drop in the bucket, a flash in the pan. Little David knew the trouble he had in front of him with Goliath. Our faith needs to be as strong as we face trouble. We are ready for the word to fight, when the time is right!" Some of our men want us to fight now and they offer up new leaders to lead in battle. These men are punished for talking against our commanders. Those that ignore orders could face death if they refuse to take commands. This is how serious things have become in the time of war.

April 10, 1836. We are going down the road to Harrisburg, where the new capitol stands. Santa Anna was just there two days ago. We know that since we are not heading east, then we must be no longer be retreating away from the Mexicans. Everyone has been in bad spirits as the watch is doubled, and fires are limited to cooking only. It was cold at night and one blanket isn't much comfort. I thought about my wife. My hope is that she hasn't cut off all her lovely hair thinking I was not coming back. It rained the rest of the night. Then no fires could be made because it was too wet. Daylight came so the clouds broke away to a fair day. One of our cannons became stuck into the mud. We tried to no avail to free it as it is quite a heavy one. We found a farm close by with some oxen that was staked by the road to graze. We asked the old woman named Widow Sarah Williams to speak with her outside since we are too muddy to come into her home. We talked with her a while to make a chance to politely ask about using her oxen. I offered to have some men fix her fence for the use of her oxen for a week or so. She agreed for the sake of her fence and five dollars! We passed the hat among the men and got two dollars and a string of glass trade beads. She scoffed at our lack of money. We are only poor soldiers, so she finally took pity on us and allowed us to take her oxen to remove the cannon from the mud. That old woman was tough as an old boot! We went away without a penny in our pockets. Still, getting that cannon back was a good idea. We may have use for it soon. It is too valuable to lose.

April 16, 1836. We break camp, and move east to Harrisburg. Our new capitol was burned to the ground by Santa Anna! The crossroads goes to Nacogdoches or Harrisburg. General Sam orders us to go to move on to Buffalo Bayou instead. "Harrisburg is a cinder, and Nacogdoches is far from where Santa Anna has gone," from what our scouts said. Now we no longer run from them! We are in in a great pursuit of them, for a change. We crossed southeast into the Buffalo Bayou to set up our camp along the northwest shore. North of us is a big swamp. To the east is the Mexican camp which is about 12 miles from us, hidden by a hill between the camps. The swamp north of us is full of snakes, alligators, and quicksand. We are partially protected. They have not discovered our camp, downwind from them. We have sent a spy to the Mexican camp to check them out." General Houston says much to us. "I will not discuss most troop movements, for the sake of secrecy, and the element of surprise. I will say that I sent two companies of soldiers to watch over things on the Brazos, two weeks ago. That is all that I can afford to move. It is just like the chess game: the wrong move and all is lost. The best element is timing: the right movement at the right time. A few days ago at Galveston Bay, our provision president David Burnet was spared by the Mexican commander Juan Almonte. President Burnet stood in the way of his wife being shot as they rowed out to the schooner named the Flash. These Mexican are an odd lot. Some are gentlemen, and some are ogres. Remember this as you deal with them! That is all I can say." The troops were seemed to be satisfied with the report as they know that we are now moving forward. Spirits lifted as we celebrated our progress.

General Houston moves to his tent to rest. He has not rested, or slept for several days, and he is unshaven. He has too much on his mind. Mister Rusk is just making more confusion to what is already difficult. He is asked to leave before sunset to take care of getting more arms, and some stout men to use them. It is for his own safety as some men here openly do not like him.

Tearing down Vince's Bridge

April 20. We are abruptly awake by General Sam beating on a copper pot with a big iron spoon like a Cherokee drum. He has not slept much in a week. He looks very tired. He has dark circles around his eyes like he was in a fight. His voice is hoarse and he can hardly speak. General Sam heard some of the new troops complain about waiting to fight, but he ignores that loose talk. General Sam washes his face in a wash basin. He drinks from the pitcher and pours the rest over his head. He combs his hair back and he drinks the coffee out of the tin pot it came in. He took a few bites of a corn cake. His color then looked better. I brought him the new reports that came in from last night. The officer of the

Day is Lieutenant Millard. He posts the new orders: the new men are made to drill, and drill some more until they get the idea down right.

We are ordered to go to Vince's Bridge to destroy it. It is the only way out of here. Deaf Smith is leading the team of men with long iron rods to pry the stones apart. The bridge is built so well it is hard to undo the stones. They swing some sledge hammers since they are so young, they have so much energy. They take turns swinging the sledges until it is just wooden bois d' arc beams left. The stones are thrown into the river. We make progress in taking it all down, but not without a few dips on the shore of the branch to cool off. We did and it was nice and deep. There was even an alligator eating a big water snake on the other bank. None of the enemy will be able to cross back over the bridge in case they are spies. They will lose their nerve to fight when we have them boxed in. We want to fight Santa Anna the same way that Cos was defeated. He will also be sent home in shame. We cannot afford to lose this fight. We get back to camp very tired, ready to eat a good meal and rest.

The new men are still having duty to perform for talking during General Sam's orders. He did not mention it to anyone but Lieutenant Millard took great note of it. He sent us to get them lined up for inspection at a moment's notice. We were in charge of them so I put them in charge of cleaning up after the horses. They then had to dig many postholes for a new fence. After it got dark the new soldiers got to eat a plate of food. They fell down to eat being too tired to stand. We felt like falling down ourselves, being tired from using the wrecking bar a day ago. Some sleep is in order after we eat a good meal. We went to read the Bible but our eyes are tired from the bright sun shining off the water.

The Trials of Training the Greenhorns

Today we have a mock battle to see how the men fare. It was hard not to laugh in their face because some were so slow to act. A terrapin would run faster than some. The tents are taken down. The supplies are being stowed away. We tried to get them pointed the right direction. Some do not know the front end of a horse from the backside. We ordered the more experienced riders to show the others how to quickly saddle their mounts. We get them all lined up and their line is crooked and lacking order. I had to walk away. Santa Anna would laugh himself to death if this group came at him! We moved back to the starting point and gave the word again to make a new crisp line. They are considerably better but they are too slow on the push to get ready. We put the more experienced men in charge of the newbies. Commander Lamar came up with his men to show us how they tend to things. Commander Goyens got a stick to draw on the ground. He took stones and pieces of bark and short sticks to represent the different cavalries and commanders. He showed us a much better choice of lines to make a better order of things. He called it a "Cherokee Stand," a solid, straight line going north and south. It will move quickly to make a line of conflict that will be hard for the enemy to escape. Commander Lamar used his left boot to kick at Commander Goyen's drawing to say he did not agree to the new tactics. He stomped the dirt to openly show contempt for another commander. Commander Millard tried to grab him to bring him to his senses. Lamar pushed him to the ground, showing him no mercy! He punched the commander in the face as he stood back up. Lamar's men openly mock the new men to kill off their morale. They also mock our commander as he is knocked to the ground. We helped the commander back up to his feet. Two wrongs do not make a right. This is not what we need as we need to make the men into a fighting force that fears no one. The men can't see us fighting each other over tactics. Commander Goyens takes out his pistol. Then he puts it back in his belt. He gave us some new orders. We moved the new men away a short ways to set their horses to graze by making a picket line, tying their horses to a single rope like a trotline. This is to show them how to secure their mounts in a safe manner. We had them rest and sit on the ground to wait for new directions once we figured out what to do next. We ordered the men not to talk at all. They are to keep their eyes watching the edge of the forest for spies and scouts for the Mexicans. Someone has been spying on us from a distance!

General Sam has been up in the tree line watching us. He rode up to do an inspection of Lamar's men and their mounts. "We are to fight the enemy, not each other!" He found that their horses needed to be washed and brushed down good. He found them in contempt of "simple respect" between officers. General Sam ordered them down to the snaky river to wash and curry their horses. Mister Lamar has to personally take down their saddles and bridles. He is in charge to make them shine with some saddle soap. His men then helped him when he became overwhelmed from the heat. This was to show the new men how it is done. Commander Lamar had some unkind words for our commanders. Once they finish their horses, then Lamar's men have to do all the horses in the picket line too. So a smart mouth does not carry much weight around here. Respect carries a high price if it is failed within our own ranks.

Trouble never ends because Widow Williams was back at the camp wanting her oxen returned so that she could plow her wheat fields. She is no Widow Lalaurie! We were nice because she is a widow, and our elder. Widow Williams is a pain in the back of the head, and worse! Again she wanted more payment or her oxen returned. General Sam was hoarse from talking so much. He confronted the woman because we need those oxen to pull the big "twin sister" cannons, so we can have more men to fight in the lines. He told her, "If Santa Anna comes our way he will take your land, your oxen, and your life if you talk to him like you do, today! Many of these soldiers have lost family, or given up much of what they have, to be here! We need these oxen to pull our cannon out of this muddy mess called the Buffalo Bayou. If we can't beat the Mexican army then we will have bigger problems than the loss of your oxen! We promise you a barrel of seed corn and the men needed to plant your fields if you will just give us some peace!" The woman just blinked hard, just like she was not hearing anything of this news. General Sam gave her his gold watch in trade, so she was appeased to finally leave. He was so relieved. So are we. He said, "I always have mercy on widows. Her poor husband had to die just to get some rest from that pushy woman!" We laughed but we tried to be polite because there might be some truth to that rumor. General Sam always has a way to deal when trouble presents itself. It comes in all shapes and sizes. Even in the form of a poor widow that is troublesome over her borrowed oxen. If he can deal with her then he can deal with whatever the Mexican army has in store for us.

The San Jacinto Battle

April 21, 1836. Our scouts come to report to us that General Cos has ships up the coast bringing 500 Mexican troops to San Jacinto to back up Santa Anna. Our advantage is fading quickly. General Sam is still asleep. It is almost mid-morning. It is the first time he has slept in over a week. Lieutenant Millard brought him his coffee. William Goyens comes in dressed in plain clothes because he is back from scouting. He has me write out a report to give General Sam. The written report is that General Cos is arriving with 500 new troops. General Sam drank down the coffee and he looked up in the sky to say a prayer. He finished, and his eyes twinkled when he saw a golden eagle flying overhead. He paused and said, "Today is the day to fight! Call the men to muster together to wait for my next orders." This is what we have been waiting for!

The horse wranglers get all the horses, and tack together for Lamar and Sherman's cavalries. The remudas we have today are much larger than any I have seen in one place! The men are asked to line up in a solid row going north and south. The line will be over two miles long! General Houston speaks loudly over the men and horses making so much noise. "We will make a 'Cherokee Stand' as our defense against the Mexicans. Our line of troops will be long and thick with infantry. The cavalry will be able to take them by surprise. Since they will have nowhere to go but into the deep San Jacinto River and into Mack Cormick's Lake. We will fight them to show them no mercy. Remember the all the men who have died at their hands! Their families have suffered greatly because of their loss. Our future lies solely with what you do today! The wind is blowing from the south and east, so the Mexican camp will not see our dust from the remuda. The wind makes the sound not carry so far. The hill between us hides us. The sun will be in their eyes if they retreat into the lake." That made sense to us as we looked at the place the sun was in the sky. It will be to our benefit if we are careful and quick. The wind picked up as it was a cool breeze blowing. I said a quiet prayer in case I do not make it. I prayed for Red Bird and that all of our army would be brave and safe.

We begin to make the line of the Cherokee Stand. Sherman's Second Cavalry is taking the northern end of the stand almost three miles east of our camp. The next part of the line is Burleson's First Infantry. Each end of his group has one of George Hockley's "Twin Sister" Cannons. The Tejanos stick a playing card or two in their hat bands so they are not mistaken for the Mexican army's wranglers. They also put on a folded red bandana around their left arm at their elbow. We will ride with Lieutenant Millard's Short Regiment led in the front by General Houston. We are ready for this battle. It is what we have trained to do for so long. There is no choice to fight, or die trying.

The most southern end of the line is Captain Lamar's Cavalry. They aren't speaking to anyone these past days. As long as they are fighting on our side, then I guess that is enough. We are to maintain a solid and unbroken line. The command was given to move slowly east and north towards the San Jacinto River. We move along at a steady pace to move toward the Mexican camp. No sudden bugle calls or loud drums are allowed. We are to march quietly to the sound of the fife and drum to keep a steady pace. They play "Will You Come to the Bower" the popular drinking song that most of the men know. The march is played softly as we approach the Mexican army camp. There are no sentries watching out. We walk into their camp without being discovered. We are all given weapons to use on the enemy. We draw out our Bowie knifes to make good use of them. A dog barks and breaks the silence. Our men yell "Remember the Alamo! Remember Goliad! Remember Zantacas!" Some of the Mexicans ran to the lake and the river to be blinded by the sun shining off it. Since Vince's Bridge is destroyed and the deep swamp north of us. They are trapped because we have them all boxed in like a rabbit.

We made our way through their camp. They are so scared they cannot do anything but perish at our hands. In a half an hour the battle is over for they are in the middle of their siesta: their rest time during the hot part of the day. It is terrible for death is all around us. We feel horrible as this is a dreadful thing! It was like seeing my own time of being near death and then seeing Delephine die. All that came back to me again. I felt sick, but relieved that all we have worked to do has finally been done. This is war and this is what the training has been about. They are but a handful of Texicans dead. Each one is a brave soul. I think I was wounded and stabbed in the arm. I was so scared I did not realize it until sometime later. There are many worse off so I help them. It is a small thing considering all of the Mexican losses. It would be us, at their hands if we had not attacked them. The men at Goliad surrendered and were unarmed. They were slaughtered like they were chickens for the dinner table. This is how we are able to do this thing as a necessary, unpleasant task. Still we take no joy in this. It was matter of time before we are part of a battle. It is better today than any other day to die. Our life is worth lying down if it means people can live in Texas, free from of harm. It would be us if it wasn't them.

We are to take stock of our losses. The Tejanos took prisoners into a grove of cedars. A perimeter of rope is tied around the trees to contain the Mexican prisoners. Our orders are to shoot anyone who crosses under the rope for whatever the reason. Our watch makes for a long day, but we finish in four hours. The 25 Mexican Tejanos in our own troop have come to taunt the prisoners. Most of them have lost some of their family at the Alamo, Goliad, or Zantacas.

Some Texicans are just hoping the prisoners to cross under the rope. A few tried and they paid the price. Some have wounds and they are moved under guard to a field next to the lake. A few have died since the battle and they are buried together with the Texans who have died earlier. Some of the men who stayed back from battle are put to work for a burial detail. A number of men lost their nerve to fight so they were pulled out of the line. They were to stay back to help guard the supplies from being ransacked by the enemy soldiers.

General Houston lay under an oak tree wounded in the left leg with his ankle busted up bad. His face is swollen from his fall from his horse after it was shot out from under him. He asked for the reports of troop numbers of the wounded and the dead. Mirabeau Lamar, the commander of the cavalry gave the tally of 630 Mexican soldiers are killed, and 730 are taken prisoner. Santa Anna has not been found among the dead, or prisoners." Four different people took count so it took a while to get a solid count for the report. General Sam looks pale and tired from pain. He manages to smile and say, "A fox always shows up, sooner or later." He then is relieved to hear that there was only nine Texans killed, and thirty wounded. The Mexican commander Juan Almonte was found to be able to address the men. Some wanted to harm him. He asked for their mercy as he showed mercy on our provisional president Burnet. General Sam asked that he have the chance to have a guard walk with him as he takes stock of what can be done to help the wounded. He is to help with the identification of the dead. He also asked about Santa Anna. In all the confusion he could be anywhere, even among the dead. "Most men on both sides are expected to survive." The order is that there is a cease fire and that no one is to be hurt or harmed unless they go to escape or harm us in some way. No one is to bully the prisoners as it was reported by Juan Almonte. The orders are given that anyone who hurts the Mexican soldiers for no good reason will be shot! In a time of war it is still needed for our people to act like they are civilized.

General Sam is tired from all the stress. His wounds are bothering him. Most medical supplies were left behind the battle lines so they would not be captured by the enemy in case we failed. All the doctors are out in the battlefield tending to those who could not be moved. General Sam needed some aid so Red Bird made him a mesquite tea from his medicine bag. He added some moonshine that one of the men offered so it was nice and stout. We wrote him out a good report to keep track of the events. I read it to Commander Goyens. He signed it before he gave it to the officer of the day, Commander Millard. We are told to rest for a few hours because we are wounded. We are told to go to the field hospital where it is some short grass on a bit of a hill. Doctor Neathery comes to look at my arm. The shot went through my arm so he poured some of that moonshine on my arm. I got sick from the pain, and the bandages soon made the pain better when the bleeding stopped and the air could not get to it. I looked around to see if I knew anyone on the field. My prayers are for both sides not to suffer any more loss. One of the new men was close by. He shot very badly. I went over to him to help him out. He then died as I was trying to comfort him. Others needed help so I went along the lines of the wounded. I brought some water to them. Then I was lightheaded because of the loss of blood. Red Bird went about helping where he could. A Mexican soldier jumped up and held a knife up to his chest. Red Bird stuck his hand into the man's wound so he dropped the knife. He had the man held down as poured salt into the man's wound to help it stop bleeding. Red Bird had a few cuts and bruises but his spirits were high because he was able to use his medicine to help so many people. Our doctors had plenty to do so he enjoyed being helpful to those that he could help.

It is hard to sleep after seeing so much destruction. The troublesome people were kept under a better watch as the moon is full. Things have to be better now. Our sacrifice has been great on both sides of this conflict. I am not sure that any good can come from all this terrible loss.

April 22, 1836. It was surprising that it was so quiet last night. The stresses of the recent battle haunt us. Our spirits have been real high, and at times real low. We slept some, but not enough. Some of the men seem angry for no real reason. The actions of the day kept going on, over and over, in my thoughts. We do not talk much to each other. It is just enough to listen to what is necessary to say. We go check on General Sam. He often asks us to take some notes for him or to help write some letters. He is in good spirits for someone shot by small rifle balls with a broken left ankle! Doctors D.E. Neatherly and Branch Archer came to look at his leg. It seems that this rifle called an "escarpito" is something called a "shotgun" the French made to shoot game birds. General Sam jokes that he must have been out 'turkey hunting' on Buffalo Bayou. Doctor Neatherly takes some of the bird shot out of General Sam. It was some terrible big brass and copper shot. He showed his leg wound. We took some wood to split it for a leg brace to wrap with some bandages It looked most terrible as some of the shot is too deep to remove out in the field. His foot and leg is in danger of being removed because of infection. He was very brave. Doctor Neatherly poured whiskey onto the wound. We held General Sam back from moving off the table. General Sam tried to use his sense of humor in the face of his bad pain. "Don't waste good whiskey on my leg when my head hurts so badly from the fall off that horse!" We poured him some whiskey to drink because he was in so much pain. It helped him as he was in need of some good medicine. Many of the field goods were ruined and lost at the last rain storm. He was in better mood as his pain was helped. "Today, we will move to Empresarrio De Zavala's home to make a field hospital for our men on one side, the wounded Mexicans on the other. They are no threat, for their spirit is broken. The Mexican soldiers are bewildered like many of us. They do not know the whereabouts of their leader Santa Anna, or if he is even alive."

By midmorning some of our soldiers have a very special prisoner: Santa Anna! He is dressed in the outfit of an irregular Mexican private. The uniform has blood on it from a bullet wound and bayonet tear. Santa Anna must have removed his uniform, traded his with a dead man by hoping to hide among the dead. He was trying to escape after we have left to tend to our dead and wounded. He thought wrong for he is now our prisoner! General Houston asked Santa Anna if he is hurt. Juan Seguin speaks to him in Spanish: "Tu padecimiento, hoy?" "Are you suffering today?" Santa Anna quietly says, "Meramente, mi orguilo!" "Merely my pride!" we are told. Juan Seguin stands between him and several members of the Texas army. Commander Seguin draws out his gun and promises trouble if anyone comes closer to the prisoner. No one gets too brave to try.

The men are ready to do away with him if he tries
anything rash. General Houston lies beneath an oak tree in

great distress. The men want to outright kill Santa Anna. General Houston said, "There has been enough killing on both sides. Enough! If he is killed, then no one will be able to take back our peace treaty. Mexico will still not recognize us as independent, even after all this death and destruction. It will not mean anything." The men quieted down their protests, realizing that General Sam is right. People are still under his command. He encourages people to have an opinion, but not to the point of disrespect of our supreme commander.

It is late night and we have got moved to the field hospital at De Zavala's home. General Sam's left leg is swollen to two times the regular size. Red Bird applies some Cherokee medicine to help the swelling go down, so a splint can be applied. It is set before the swelling becomes too bad. We had his leg raised up to allow it to swell less. He would not be still for long so we had to encourage him to rest. His leg stayed swollen so they all had a time to make him more comfortable. There were mass burials for those that died from both sides. General Sam ordered that proper respect be shown for the dead with prisoners being allowed to help with the burial details.

April 26. Thirty-five Mexican wounded are still our prisoners. Some are now stable enough to be moved a short ways in a wagon, to where they can watch the burials. Commander

Lamar wanted all the prisoners to be moved to where they can be penned up in a dark stockade. Doctor Neatherly protested greatly. He was usually a quiet person that seldom spoke above what is tolerated. "Some prisoners are so weak that they will die if they are moved too far!" Last week the able prisoners were made to travel to San Antonio in smaller groups that are easier to control. Commander Goyens was in charge of the wounded of both sides. He kept Mister Lamar at bay with orders for him not to harass the wounded prisoners. He pulled out his pistol to show his contempt for Mister Lamar. He put his pistol back into his belt and he held his peace. If looks could kill, we would be short a commander for our cavalry! Mister Lamar was put on a new duty to take a patrol south to look for Mexican "scragglers": escaped enemy soldiers that might be a problem to the settlements if they take a notion to cause trouble. There were none that we knew of, but just in case there were any. He was just sent away for the sake of his good health!

The Tejanos that fought against Santa Anna have become part of the force that is to be taken to Victoria and Galveston. General Sam is to go to New Orleans to have his wounds seen about for we fear that he may lose all his left leg. He is a strong person, so he will survive either way. The people around him have a time to keep him safe from trying to do too much. We doubled the guard to keep him safe.

Since he was hurt he felt the need to be protected as he had threats against him by some that felt "he had waited too long to fight."

Tonight we read Psalm 117, "Praise."

The Runaways return

Monday, April 27, 1836. The big news spreads of our success at the Battle of San Jacinto. The hero of the day is "Sam Jacinto" as many people now called General Houston. We are able to travel to Groce's plantation after getting some rest. A mass exodus of settlers is coming back to their homesteads. We are ready for them this time! They will not be the same trouble that they were before. Commander Goyens laid down the law last time, so the word has spread as well over our recent victory. We rode all day as we have orders to keep things civilized. Also new settlers are coming since we have done all the hard work. They are gutless to want a land grant as they have done nothing to earn it as we have. These might be the real troublemakers in our future days.

April 28. The rivers are down this time. There is not the pressure that was before of the Mexicans attacking, so there is a more gradual return to their farms. The farms need tending to. Most of the fields are in a mess, the cattle are all scattered. The people have also arrived to give aid to fight. They are late for the fight but they will be able help tend our cattle and fields, since they are so willing to help us. These people have been gathered together to help the people affected by the "Run Away Scrape". Things will be put back into order, roads will be fixed, and farms will be tended. These men might not have to fight, but they will earn their land with their sweat and toil like we have. No "greenhorn" will come here and get an easy break as we have suffered more than some, to the point of death. The new men will have to hunt and help those that can't because they are widows. Shooting at game is not the same as someone shooting at you. The price is high in Texas for land. Blood has been spilled so that warrants much respect.

The Tejanos have been our best allies. They have been the ones that kept the Mexicans in check by their good help and support of our army against Mexico! We have been able to be free to keep our army busy taking care of the details of things. We have been very busy from sunrise to sunset. We have the new men dig latrines for the officers and now for ourselves. I am strong enough now to give orders and get some things done. Still, I missed my wife and I longed to be with her. I looked at the picture that I drew of her. It helped me not be so lonesome for her. We will wait a while longer to see her. It won't be long before we see our Cherokee family in the Piney Woods! It will be worth the wait to get back to a simple way of life. My son is to be born soon, and Red Bird will be a father too. So we have good reason to survive this fight. Red Bird said that he will teach his new son to be a medicine chief as he grows up. His chance of being a new father means the world to him. We talk about hunting and farming cornfields that would be the envy of any tribe.

CHAPTER SEVEN

The New Texican Government Begins

After San Jacinto things have been so different! The people that have badmouthed us so terrible in past are now praising us like we could do no wrong! David Burnet is still to be the temporary president until there could be an election. Then they praise us for our victory over Santa Anna's splintered army. There was a roster of wounded and dead from the Alamo, and Goliad battles added to the names of those killed at San Jacinto. Letters are being written to their families praising them for their bravery and valor in protecting Texas from being taken back by Mexico. All of us who can write are ordered to do so to help out. Our regular duties are suspended until we can write letters to the families of the dead and the wounded. We are given a list to names and the towns where their families can be reached. We have a basic form the letters take to make them acceptable. We leave a place at the bottom where General Sam can sign them. We signed our name on a small place lower than the place we left blank for General Sam. We have one more day to write proper letters and to read the letters that others have written so that we know they are proper to send out. There were many names and it was sad to do this chore. General Houston was praised most of all for his bravery, and wisdom in leading the Texans against great odds with the battle against the Matamoros, and Guerrero Battalions!

Doctor Anson Jones consulted with Doctor Branch T. Archer. Doctor D.E. Neatherly came from tending to the Mexicans that were close to death. He is seeing the color and the mess that was once General Houston's left shin and ankle bones. They recommended that General Houston take the next ship to New Orleans. He is to have his left leg fixed by a surgeon that had a better hospital and more skill. General Houston has suffered with terrible pain and headaches since his horse Star was shot out from under him. The fall from his horse did not help him any, as did his leg from that escarpito wound. General Sam was relieved from command by General Rusk. He was happy to be relieved from the burden of command for a while. We went into his tent and welcomed him with some fresh corncakes that the local women have made today. He was pleased to see us and he showed us what project that he was working on. He seemed delighted that someone else held the reins for a while. He unrolled a number of maps to show us the progress being made with the Republic Road. He was in a sunny mood talking about the first graded road going from Waco to the Red River! He said that this road was the first real sign of progress. He said that making Texas a good place to live was going to take some real work, and a great deal of planning. We have our work cut out for us to make some progress here!

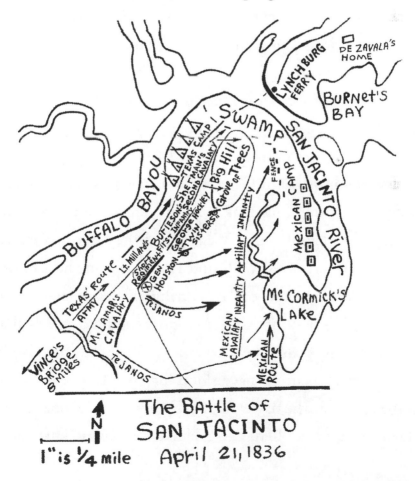

The Battle of SAN JACINTO
April 21, 1836

1" is ¼ mile

N

The Late Bloomers

All these people that have come here too late to fight need to be kept busy so they will not add to our problems! The people that just arrived here have a great deal of energy that needs to be put to some good use. We need some relief, for we are still weary from all the stress of battle, even before the fight. General Sam asked if I would ride with him with a detachment of men to Galveston. He was in a talking mood so I told him that I would go. I told Red Bird that I was going to ride with General Houston to Galveston. He sent word back with some soldiers' wives going to Fort Houston so the wife would not worry too much. He said that they would have her stay with them in the barracks while I was gone. He will keep an eye on things, and keep some of my chores caught up so I would not be too far behind on things. We left at sunrise with General Sam. His wagon was made special with springs that make the rough roads not so terrible, as a regular wagon would. We stopped the wagon every 12 miles to rest the horses. We found a cool watering hole to rest by during the hot time of day. During our rest General Sam unrolled a big map of east Texas. He says that he feels that the Trinity River could be used as a trade route as the Caddo and Cherokee Nations have done for over 100 years. Deaf Smith has spent the past week on Cypress Bayou looking for a boat route to the Red, and Mississippi Rivers! This could

be a quick way to get goods from the Federal States. We want
to be prepared for war in case it comes back again.

We stopped at a house along the way that allows
people to stay to rest a few hours to have something to eat.
I showed General Sam my map of the battle. He told me
a few details that I missed. I drew a copy of it for his use.
I put it on a window light to get the best details to show
through the paper. He liked the finished work. He thanked
me for being helpful as often he felt that some people around
him did and said things that hurt him. He has been through
much before being wounded. Now he doubts if peace can be
made possible. Worse of all: General Sam fears losing his left
leg, and his good health. I asked him if he was running for
president of Texas. He drank a big swallow of water, and he
put some over his face from the dipper. He smiles his friendly
smile, and he says that he will have to see how his health is
doing when he gets back from New Orleans about a month
from now. He says that he is amazed by the number of people
that have come here since Mexico has backed down from
attacking us, for the time being. Still it does not take much
to stir up a hornet's nest. We will have to wait to see what
Cos and the other generals have in mind. We have stirred up
a hornet's nest, so now we have to deal with them the best
we can.

Galveston and the Brutus

General Sam was tired and short tempered with the newcomers that just arrived here. We are waiting for the arriving ship called the Brutus. After it comes it has to be unloaded. He was anxious about such a big crowd gathered around him. He said, "Where were all these people when we needed them, a few months ago?" I said for him to not blame himself for those that died at the Alamo, and Goliad. "We won our fight against that terrible Santa Anna! General Cos was not able to muster his forces against us after we defeated him a year ago when he attacked San Antonio and held up in the Alamo. We have achieved a solid peace in Texas." General Sam said, "We should have destroyed that fortress when we had a chance! We cannot let our guard down until Mexico accepts our peace treaty, and sees us as independent from them. Until then, General Cos can come back to plague us looking for revenge for San Jacinto! General Cos might be the least of our problems! I will have to run for president. I pray to be healed, so I can get off on the right foot in dealing with our growing pains. If our government goes broke, we will have even bigger problems! Our tax burden from Mexico has just about broken all those that have tried to make a living farming. That is why so many Mexicans joined the Tejanos in our fight against Santa Anna." We need people that are determined to fight like they do! We all have a stake in our Independence." We set back to riding. We will reach

Port Galveston by nightfall. It is a busy place full of ships, and people.

Tonight we read: AMOS, Chapter 3. "God's Discipline shows His Love."

General Houston leaves for New Orleans

May 1, 1836. General Sam gets ready to leave Galveston for New Orleans. This morning there was a large crowd of people gathered to see General Sam off. Waiting here were a large group of over 100 men that have just arrived on the ship called the Brutus. General Sam limped about sizing up the group of men. These men came to Texas looking for a fight. General Sam told them to get behind a plow, and help gather all the loose livestock and horses together.

A few of the men mocked General Houston. He stayed very calm. He told them to do as he asks for this is the best way to help us! The men said that they were looking for something more exciting than rounding up a herd of someone else's cows. They could have stayed home and done the same thing. General Houston said, "If you men are not helping us you would just be hindering us by being in the way. Strangers here with nothing to do will just have time on their hands to get into trouble! If the men have come here to get land grants they will need to learn to take orders, for land grants require three years' service in the army!" The men listened to reason realizing that General Sam was right. Commander Fannin came up about that time to make a duty roster for the new men to follow. We wished General Sam well, and parted company with Commander Fannin's new troops. The new men got signed up. We traveled back to San Jacinto. The trip back went fast from all the company we have. We are to go to Groce's Plantation to take the new men to their training. We have a tough row to hoe because General Cos still threatens us! Threats grow old as we can only be threatened for so long. Now we can have a chance for peace because we have no revenge left in our hearts. All we can think about is getting back home and farming again with our new family.

Tonight, we read: Deuteronomy Chapter 6, Verse 5. "The Great Commandment."

The Velasco Treaty is drawn up

May 12, 1836. David Burnet has come to draw up the Mexican peace treaty. He is to go to Velasco tomorrow, after reviewing the new troops. Secretary of War William Rusk officially takes the reins of command from General Houston while he recovers in New Orleans. A petition signed by 2,500 men is brought before President Burnet. He is alarmed by all the fuss. Mister Burnet reads the petition out loud. The men are demanding that General Rusk to take revenge for all the lives that have been lost at the hands of Santa Anna, and Cos. The men also demand that Santa Anna be executed for war crimes done for executing the soldiers that surrendered at Goliad and at the Alamo. Santa Anna is compelled to sign the treaty, we heard. To do otherwise might be risky for his future, according to some. We are tired of all the details that try to fix this bad situation here. The treaty is detailed so it is up to them to fix this problem treaty in a peaceful way.

June 10, 1836. General Rusk is sending the new troops to Victoria to see that the Mexican troops are leaving for home. They still have not all moved out for some wounded will stay behind. Moving them would kill them on the way home. General Sam told President Burnet that he expects no more death, on either side for it would wreck the peace process. General Houston is not to be doubted now, for all their new prospects will come from the threat of Mexico being less without Santa Anna. Our chance to settle on our own land has more of a real chance now. It seems like a dream come true. We have come so far in just a year.

We are given a month's leave at Galveston

June 12, 1836. General Rusk gives us our orders that we will stay at Port Galveston until General Houston returns. We are then told that our wives are to meet us, and keep us company until General Sam returns, in about three weeks! We have earned a decent rest. The stresses of all the past months are telling on us. We are ready to see the ocean. The Gulf of Mexico is lovely to see. It is better with someone sweet as the wife, and time to enjoy it.

June 14. We arrive at Galveston. We are given great treatment since we have fought at San Jacinto. We are not allowed to pay for any food, or lodging. The people at Galveston would not hear of it. We are given new clothes, since all we have is our military clothes. We are given two smart looking shirts, and a pair of summer pants. We get all cleaned up to look sharp when our wife gets here. By eight at night we met our loved ones and we dance around like it is Christmas. What a wonderful sight! All we have been put through lately seemed to melt away, at the sight of Say-te-Qua. She is wonderful as the stars at night, and the sunrise in the morning! She is heavy with child, but she never looked so beautiful! This is what I have been fighting for.

General Houston returns

July 3. General Houston is to return today. He arrives on the ship called "The Brutus" recently built and named well. General Sam walked slowly with a cane, and has a bit of a limp when he walks. He is happy. His color is very good. He looks better than he has in a long time. This was the some good news for our friend to come back in good spirits and better health. We look better too, for seeing our loved ones was the best medicine. We are greeted by General Sam. People are all around him. We finally get to talk to him to tell him how good it is to see him doing so well. He is going back to Nacogdoches to settle down and make plans for the future. He freed two slaves that now work for him as hired help. He was pleased to do what is right to do.

Tonight, we read Psalms 117, "Praise."

July 5, 1836. General Houston calls together all the men who fought in San Jacinto. We get a paper that states we have fought in the Mexican War, and that we are worthy of a land bonus for serving in the army. The widows of the Texans who have served and died will be given land for their loss. We have to wait until we have finished our military service before we can homestead our land. Three years will seem like a long time to wait. Our duty to our Lord and family comes first. We are anxious to settle down as soon as possible, before all the good water, and pasture land is gone. Many more settlers are coming in some are green and wild as new persimmons. We are to police the new comers to make them aware of the rules concerning the boundaries, and proper trade with the Red River tribes.

A true peace starts with us

July 11, 1836. Red Bird and I are to go to the Hacienda of Lorenzo De Zavala, our field hospital where the twelve wounded Mexican soldiers have been staying until they are healed well enough to travel. We are here to give them aid, some letters, and packages from their home. We felt that we owed them an act of Christian kindness. Since they are our sworn enemy, but we no longer hold any harm or anger against them. We wish to understand each other better. The only way to a real peace is by the hand of friendship, and humility. We have seen how the Caddo and Cherokee have made treaties. They now trade horses, and wild cattle for a rich barter. It is preferred over fighting. They are good trade partners with most of the Louisiana border tribes. This is what we model our peace plan after. They will bring word of our planned peace treaty to others in Mexico.

Today, we will serve the Mexicans a good meal. We give them letters from home, and presents. A warrior is worthy of great respect. There is no place in our heart for revenge. We show the Mexican prisoners concern by showing them some simple kindness to shake their hand and tell them that we are honorable men like Juan Almonte when he spared David Burnet and Hanah, his wife. We have no bad feelings, for they are only following the orders from a tyrant under the threat of death to their families if they failed to follow through. We are here because it is our duty as Christians, not just as soldiers to be fair in our treatment of each other. This will help us have peace between us and avoid all this unnecessary killing. The Mexican men are visibly shaken, because they went from being fearful of us as enemies. Some of our men have treated them bad since they have been our prisoners. It is easier being a brother that is interested in their wellbeing. We would have rather went down that path, in the first place! The Cherokee taught me that by the way they took me in. We could all be enemies, but now there is no reason to hate them. We gave each of the men their letters and gifts from some family. Red Bird talked to them in Spanish to explain our reason to be there. Tejanos Vicente Cordova, and Carlos De La Garza arrived to help the men get the news told to them where they would understand things better. They showed an open right hand to show that they had no offensive weapons. Captain Cordova said to the wounded prisoners in Spanish, "Por Usted, mi hermanos: Soy una amigo! Usted no desconocido para mi, hoy. (pause) Hace lectras, Y paquettes desde tu familia!" "For you, my brothers: I am your friend! You have no fear of me today. Here are letters and packages from your families!" The prisoners looked relieved as one stated that he thought that they were going to be shot like the soldiers at Goliad. Captain De LaGarza said, "Desembarazo por Usted en una semana! Ser muy feliz!" "Freedom for you: sirs! In just a week! Be happy!" It was like Christmas for them because they now know that they will be given safe passage to go home as soon as the doctors determine they are safe to travel. They cry openly and they are beside themselves from all the good news. These men will be our true peace ambassadors when they return home safely. Peace is now possible if the Velasco Treaty is accepted, and Santa Anna is to be released soon. General Sam talked about this as did the Tejanos as we sat back and watched the men from a distance. We left the men to enjoy their presents and their letters from home. A jug of moonshine was found by the Tejanos. They had taken it from an unruly soldier, so some was poured into gourd cups for the men to enjoy as part of their celebration. It was well-earned as they have suffered some stress as prisoners. Even before this they were threatened with death by their former commanders if they failed to fight or travel fast enough to battle! We will leave out with them tomorrow to go to Galveston. We will pray for them to be well as we leave out together, so early in the morning.

Tonight we read Job 31, "Pride."

Commander Lamar takes the reins

July 22, 1836. The Mexican General Urrea is at Matamoros, building up a large force demanding the release of Santa Anna from prison! The 155 Tejanos that fought against him have today brought a new petition to have Santa Anna freed.

The Treaty of Velasco has to be accepted by the Mexican government! The Tejanos are ready to have the treaty accepted, and put into action. They all fear if someone harms Santa Anna, the whole peace process will be ruined. Many members of the Texas army fear that Mexico will be hard to control once Santa Anna is freed. President Burnet is naming Mirabeau Lamar, from the cavalry to replace General Rusk. He is not quite able enough to handle the army since he is not General Sam. Commander Lamar gets less respect of the men than General Rusk, or General Sam does. His hardnosed attitude was difficult to deal with most days. Some of the men refuse his leadership so he loses his temper. Many have strong words for all of us for allowing the men in the ranks to bad mouth him, and refuse his leadership. We can only put so many on guard duty and Kitchen Patrol. This is not so good for us. He will make things more difficult for us all since he has been ready to command since he got here. We have little time to rest and it seems as busy as it was back at Groce's. These new men are the troublesome lot as they have no respect for any authority. They fight each other like a bunch of silly boys over a toy.

We have to read reports about the threats of General Urrea to Commander Lamar. He laughs and he mocks the words of the report. "If we were wise we would just kill Santa Anna and varnish that Velasco treaty on the coffin lid." I was horrified by his words. I just stared at him as I could not believe that this man was a commander. First governor Smith, and now this commander Lamar! Where does it stop from here? I continued with my reports as I was required to do. I left as soon as I could get away. Later I tried to sleep but I could not.

The Army gives their vote for Felix Hutson from Mississippi. President Burnet is at odds with the army for going against his orders. He has changed the date of the election to be moved up four months earlier than planned. He fears that the Texas army may be so strong that it may try to take over the new government! These new men are hungry to grab some land and they would kill each other for the chance to get it. We have created a bad thing here, like a horse that won't take to the reins! A maverick that is better off dead. It would only cause destruction to all that are around us if it is left to its own devices.

September 28, 1836. The vote for president will be taken soon. This will make the government stronger. Once people are voted into office, rather than assigned to their positions. Earlier notions were feeble: for our governor and a few commanders we had. Some are just not being popular with the majority of people no matter what they do. The new arrivals have their own notions since the dust is beginning to settle in Texas. General Sam needs to return and soon!

August 1, 1836. We are about to hear the presidential candidates speak today at Nacogdoches on the town square. They have hopes of being president of Texas, especially Temporary President Burnet. He feels that he would be a good candidate, since he has been doing such a good job. Many people in the army say that he should not pat himself on the back too quickly, for they feel that are other more worthy candidates. We will listen to make up our own mind if General Sam does not return in time. The debate started early for it will be so hot today. The candidate Henry Smith spoke next. He said that since he has been governor that he already understands policy, and politics. People threw potatoes when he got up to speak. He should be the man that shovels out the horse stalls because he only gets a small majority of people to his camp. Smith could have accepted the Mexican Federal's help so we could have stopped Santa Anna much sooner. Most people are not convinced that he is able. That is why we are here to size up the candidates, and see where they stand on the important issues. This is my first time to vote so I am excited.

OUR COMMANDER COL. STEPHEN F. AUSTIN

Empresarrio Stephen F. Austin speaks next. He is backed by Doctors Branch Archer and D.E. Neatherly who are also well respected. Mister Austin has a large following since he has settled over 100 families to Texas. Many of them are not able to vote, for they look like a minority of people: most too young to vote and some are women who can't vote. Robert Williamson walks up to the speaker stand on his crutch. He balanced his leg on top of a wooden leg because of a bullet wound. His right leg is still attached below the knee, but he cannot walk on it without being in a lot of pain. It was most odd but he is still a reasonable person. His movement across the stand took away from his words. Next is William Wharton, the "Old Texians" as a past member of the "War Party" with Colonel Jim Bowie. His words echo Williamson's speech. He wants to protect the ranchos, and Spanish land grants that have first been in place, from being divided up into pieces, by the new settlers homesteading land that already has a previous owner. He spoke strong for half an hour. There was a lot of banter, back and forth, debating the rights of earlier settlers, and the rights of the new homesteads.

Mister William Wharton finishes up his speech. About this time General Sam arrives on his Sorrow, Maggie. All the earlier words are like they have been washed away by the rain. The crowds of people start yelling for General Sam. "Sam Jacinto, Sam Jacinto!" His horse Maggie is calmed, for we do not want General Sam hurt. He slowly climbs down, and takes his cane to help him walk. The people did not stop yelling their approval for General Houston. The victory at

San Jacinto did more than any words can say. The people cheered, and talked something fierce. The General said, "Need I say more? I think you have said it for me!" The crowd went crazy, for they adore him. His actions, not just his words speak well. Since General Sam had waited to announce his running for President. Unlike many candidates: he has not worn out his welcome with empty promises. He did not get up and argue or bad mouth the other candidates. He just has to show up on his horse, and that was all he had to do! He did not have to say anything more. The people cheered for him. That said it all.

September 4, 1836. The election was held three days ago. The results are not too surprising: Colonel Austin is defeated since he backed President Burnet not going into Mexico. This has set badly with many people. They voted their convictions, by keeping some people out of office. Since they are slow to get Texas as independent from Mexico, they do not hear the wishes of the people, so the people have to elect someone who would listen to their concerns and address them. The vote was counted three times to make sure of the results. President General Houston gets 5,110 votes. Governor Smith, 743 votes. Colonel Austin split the vote, with 587 votes, so Governor Smith could not get a majority to win. Put together they would not be able to win. To get such a clear win means that it will put an end of debate over who rules around here. The vote for vice president went to Mirabeau B. Lamar the head of the San Jacinto cavalry. He wins over Alexander Horton. Secretary of War, Thomas Rusk do not get a majority in their favor. Things will be better since the dust has finally settled since the vote was counted three times and made valid. Now we can get things done. We are still in danger by being divided in our loyalties here.

September 15, 1836. We are making preparations for fixing up our town for the Inaugural celebration, over a month away. During all the debates and arguing over politics, there has been much tore up around here. People pulled up fences, and tore up all the hitching posts, along the Main Street. We got some post hole diggers, some bois d' arc post, and some three penny nails. We have many men set to digging and putting things back as part of our plan. There are enough rowdy men that have too much time on their hands. Enough men have been placed on guard duty. Many newcomers are set to make this a decent place to live again. It is no place like Jefferson, but in time it may just be close to it. Some of these farm boys think that since the big battles are over that this is nothing left to do but drink and fight each other! We could have used some of that "stubbornness" much early on as we were sorely lacking some men with such a need to fight someone so bad.

September 17, 1836. We continue to make progress to put some white wash on the new fence made of sawmill lumber. This is a nicer looking place to live now, and hopefully it will stay that way.

We see General Sam talking to a big group of people. We all get to ask him one question and that is all. My turn finally comes. "What do we call you now: 'General Sam' or President Sam Houston?" He smiles and laughs. He says, "Whatever you call me, know that I am working for the best interest of Texas, Texicans, and Texians. Old and newcomers alike: we are all now called Texans! One people: who now have a great future. Your confidence in me is securely placed as someone who cares to do what is proper for our prosperity here."

January 10, 1837. New orders arrive today. We are to go back to Fort Houston. We are to leave Commander Johnston in the care of the doctor at Galveston. We encourage Mister Johnston to survive this turmoil. We understand his great distress at the hands of others. I have him given him into the best of a doctor's care. I have written a report to give to President Houston. Commander William Goyens comes to get us to go. We will go back to the business of trading horses. This sounded good to me for a change is sorely needed.

We outlook has been down as we miss our home with the Cherokee in east Texas.

January 28, 1837. We get back to the fort to find that the family barracks has doubled in size since that so many people have come here to get their own land. The new buildings have been supplemented by many wall tents. We find that some men were happily to sign up for land, but not so happy to have to fight to earn it. We risk our lives to live here, so they are no better than us. The chance to settle along the new Red River settlements is just worth taking the risk to do it.

February 1, 1837. A cold north wind has come in today. We have been tending the horses by keeping plenty hay for them to eat. My horse, Radish, has had the colic bad. She seems like she needs better medicine than I know. I need to be tended to better because I can't see straight when I first wake up. I sat in by her stall to try to feed her but she will not eat. She may have eaten something bad, or some poison. We got some charcoal and chopped it up, and put it in with some nice oats so she would eat it. Charcoal and a little cane syrup to entice her to swallow it all. She finally sniffed the oats, and gulped it all down like a kid with candy. She seems to be doing better since she started drinking out of the trough again. She has a chance now to prosper.

February 2, 1837. I spent another long, cold night in the barn. It was worth it to see Radish her stubborn self again. Say-te-Qua said that she has stomach problems. She wonders if she has to become a horse to get any attention around here. I told her that I would get the charcoal and cane syrup, if she would get the oats! She was not happy at that request. I stay gone away too long, doing my army duty. I do not spend enough time with her to be like a married couple should be. I told her that horses do not hold a candle to her. We got cleaned up and dressed up well. I took her to eat at a nice place where there was dancing and a play that told about a married couple trying to get along. It was better than any medicine as it was just what we both needed. She needed more of my time and effort. I sincerely apologized for I have been very foolish as I have been quite a stupid man and a poor husband. A Qualls will tell you what they think and then some. She has been very patient so I will do better to show her more respect and slow down on my plans without telling her first and asking her own ideas and notions like any "good chief" would.

Tonight we read First CORINTHIANS, Chapter 13. "The Love Chapter."

February 14. The cold weather has turned fair this week. We are glad to get out and stomp around. We got out and hunted two geese. We shot at five, but only got close to these two. We have grown fat and lazy so our aim is not better than it once was. The cooking pot looked empty, and we can use the feathers to make us each a nice pillow to sleep on. One goose is given to the Widow Holmes, for her table. She is most pleased to be provided for. She makes the best pies and cobblers from the fruit she cans in glass jars. She lost her husband at San Jacinto so we are to look in on her to help her do some of the more difficult chores. She has made a peach cobbler that she sends home with me. It was still warm from the oven. I hope it makes it home with me.

March 1, 1837. The past two weeks, there has been a steady trail of wagons coming here to settle. The Land Office has not opened yet, for there is still no one to run it "officially". The land scripts of a square mile are to be homesteaded for at least three years. The land has to be planted by the second growing season to allow for cabins and barns to be put up. Groups of five women or more have come to get a single lot of "single" land, in hopes of finding a single man, and a future. The corral is full of oxen, and the wagons are filling up the wagon barn. People have called President Houston to open the Land Office. He has yet to pick someone who would be fair to run it. This fort has become a big town in just a year. They are adding to the size of fort to make more lodging for travelers and visitors. We find that there are even bigger concerns to tend to here: Some of the settlers have brought slaves to help break the land, and to help plant! This is not the Texas we fought for! It does not set well with a lot of people who want slavery to stop at the Red, and Sabine Rivers. At the church services the preacher talks about the spread of the "Evil of Slavery." There are several parishioners that do not like has words. It leaves a bad taste in their mouth. They are cut to the quick as they do not like to hear the truth. So they get up during the sermon. The preacher stops to criticize them for being rude. He tells them to all repent. The invitation comes quickly to accept Christ at the end of the sermon. They ignore him, and continue to leave out. The majority of people stay to pray and be open to the message. The preacher says, "We just saw the wheat separated from the chaff, just like during the Rapture!" It is good to see that people stick by their convictions, even if they are wrong. They are being convicted of their sin by their actions. Slavery has no place in Texas as it will be a plague against us!

We read Revelation Chapter 20, Verse 2. "The War on Satan".

The Texican government survives the first year

March 2, 1837. The first anniversary of the Texan Constitution is today. It is fair and warm for this time of year. It is a far cry from how cold it was last year, at Washington, on the Brazos. Today we can go outside without a coat. President Houston is here to dedicate the new fort named after him. He said this: "First a city named Houston, then a Fort. That makes for a good birthday present. We are making some real progress here!" He mentioned his plan for

the future Republic Road. His speeches are shorter today for he is in a jovial mood. There is a big celebration, some Mexican fireworks, and a dance. There was a big debate about the Land Office. President Houston said that "This is a celebration, not a debate! All in good time: all these things are being dealt with due respect… Now let us celebrate!" A man on the guitar, and two fiddlers played a new song called "The Texas Waltz." General Sam dances slowly and carefully with his wonderful wife, Margret. Others joined in and soon the dance floor was a busy place. A young man played on a drum to keep the beat steady.

The debate faded as soon as the music started. There are games, a cake walk, and lots of good distractions. They play late into the night. We enjoyed the good food, and some good company. Hard work deserves a decent reward now and then. I got over my nerves to dance with my good wife. She laughed at my attempt to dance along with the music. My two left feet kept stepping on hers. She was polite and patient as I tried to get into step. She danced and she showed me a thing or too. She really showed some of the other dancers how it is really done! People on the dance floor stopped dancing as they then moved back to watch her dance a wonderful dance. It is a dance that the Cherokee do for special occasions like today. People clapped. President Houston gave her praise in Cherokee. He tells the others that this was done to honor this special day. Slower music plays so we can dance together much better. I held her close enough to feel her heartbeat. I then remembered why I married her in the first place. Those big brown eyes make me forget what my name is! She is so beautiful. She is soon to have our baby. Her face just glows from being so happy! Our time apart was much too long. Now we have earned our chance to be together for the rest of our lives. We never know how long that will be, so we live each day like it is our last.

PROLOGUE

The Birth of a Son

Our new orders are to travel back to Fort Houston, three days away. We are given a full week to get there as the rainy weather has set in. Red Bird and Ke-Ke have the news that she is also expecting a baby in about a month. Say-te-Qua is ready to give birth because she has trouble getting comfortable no matter what she does, or how she sits. The rain continues so we have to rest at a cabin that we come to because the Neches River is flooded. We ask the man that lived there if we could stay at their cabin since it was too bad to travel. The man told us to go away and for us to leave. The man's wife stopped him because she saw that Say-te-Qua and Ke-Ke both will have a child soon. Also we are the soldiers that saved their bacon from Santa Anna's wrath! We are to stay in the barn to have our child. It seems that Say-te-Qua is about to have our child from her terrible pain. I have never seen her so miserable so I am glad to have some kind of roof over our head. She squeezed my hand and she told me how much she enjoyed dancing at the celebration. It was a dance that celebrates a new life. The wife of the cabin owner came out here because she is a midwife by trade. It was a matter of chance to be here on such a rainy day. If we would have been on the trail we would have to make a brush arbor. The barn was nice as any council house and drier than a teepee. There was no shame in sleeping in a dry barn. The wife asked us to go outside to the barn because we are in the way. I knew she was right because I stutter too much.

We went and chopped some wood for a fire so the midwife could boil some water. We managed to find some dry wood off a tree limb growing under an overhang of the barn. The limb was dead so it was dry enough to burn. I sawed off the limb and chopped the wood up for good kindling. Red Bird came back with four rabbits he killed. He had them ready to put over the fire. Once the rabbits started cooking the husband came out of his cabin to see what smelled so good. He brought more dry wood from the overhang of dog-trot where it was stacked well. This kept us out of the way of the women and it gave us a chance to pay them for their kindness for giving us shelter here in the storm. He apologized for being so rash by judging us so harshly. Strangers have been there many times causing trouble, so they did not know us from Adam. The wash pot was now boiling on the bigger fire. He carried the pot to the door of the barn and knocked on it. His wife came and took the pot inside to made use of it. She asked us to boil one of those rabbits in a stew to make some broth. I took a pot out of the wagon to get the rabbit cooking to make the broth to keep the women strong. While that boiled we had a chance to talk and tame any misunderstanding since we got off on the wrong foot with each other much earlier. He apologized because many outlaws and desperate men have stolen from them over the past months. I told him my story then he apologized even more. I told him I understood his problems too as I have lived this over and over again blaming myself.

Red Bird stayed back as I told this man named John about our life in the army this past year. He then had even more respect for us. Red Bird brought us a cooked rabbit and offered him the first meal off of it. He took his knife and divided it up well between us. We ate well when we waited for the baby to come. John told me that his crops and cattle had been stolen twice and his barn was burned. That story sounded familiar to me. I just stayed quiet to listen as he spoke of his life in Texas. We head a baby cry. Ke-Ke came outside to tell us about the baby being a boy! She walked like a duck because she was getting so big. Her time is coming soon. Ke-Ke told me that Say-te-Qua was fine and that the baby is wonderful. She asked for me to go to the wagon to get the cradle board that they have been working on for months. This was made of nice reeds and vines woven together like a basket. It was covered in white

buckskin for a boy child to celebrate the first baby. I hurried to get it to her so I could see him. We finally got to see him after he was cleaned up for his first visit to us. He is quite big for a newborn! He looked to be over six months old! He was all of 12 pounds from what I could see! He has so much hair for a newbie! It is no wonder why she was so uncomfortable. He is bound up like a good Indian baby as all the tribes do. He looked like he was in a big parfletch. Tears went down my face because it was so wonderful! I kissed Say-te-Qua. She told me that his name is Josiah after the name in a Bible story that she likes. I was so proud that I felt that I was going to bust. Red Bird danced around because he is a proud uncle. His turn to be a father comes soon, in about a month by what the midwife named Ruth told us. We brought them the broth so that they can be strong since they have not eaten anything for a while. Say-te-Qua cried for a short time. I cried too because for the first time I was really happy. It was all worth it to see this day. If today was my last day on earth, then it was all worth it to see this child born. We have left Eden to find that evil has lost its grip on us. When I came here I suffered much death and seen our worst fears realized on the battlefield. Now a new life shines bright with all the hope in the world. We now have the knowledge of good and evil: for once good has the upper hand. For now on our life will be what we have always dreamed.

Present day

The wife finished reading to her husband. She closed the journal and put it on the book shelf. She looked down at the other three unread journals. "We have much to learn from this man. He has lived an amazing life. We thought that we learned it all in school! This auction was a good investment after all!"

The story continues with The Return to Babylon.

GLOSSARY FOR THE ESCAPE FROM EDEN
Unfamiliar Texan Terms of the 19th century

A

abolitionist: A person that was against slavery, and the spread of slavery, or human bondage. In Texas it was members of an organization called, "TABOR." Many churches were against slavery. Only 1 in 5 white settlers owned slaves. These were mostly "newcomers" who arrived later (1849) in the process of settlement. Many original, early settlers abhorred slavery, and it was when California, and Oregon, Kansas, and Nebraska were added to the Union of Federal States that the question of Slave Free States was an issue. Churches such as the historic Lonesome Dove, (that the author's family belonged to) allowed people of other races to belong. Andrew was a free slave, his wife and brother, and sister-in- laws were Cherokee. This was the plan to make a more viable settlement that allowed good Christians of all races to belong. (All God fearing Christians of those days hated slavery.) Also it was not "needed" as most families were quite large in those days, and there were plenty of helping hands to do all the chores. One in five whites owned slaves in the United States by 1860. Before that it had become unpopular in most states as many families had as many as 10 children to do all the chores around a farm.

Adai: a Louisiana tribe that is part of the Caddo confederacy.

Antonio Lopez de Santa Anna: General Santa Anna. He was dictator and ruler over Mexico during the years of the Texas republic, and the time of the Mexican wars. A year before the Texans being massacred at the Alamo Mexican General Cos had taken refuge in the Alamo. He was captured and removed as a prisoner. This caused the ire of Santa Anna looking for revenge.

He was known as the "Napoleon of the West." He was the head of the Mexican army. He was released after he made the Treaty of Velasco in 1836. He was sent back to Mexico with the intent to deliver the treaty. Instead it backfires. Santa Anna said, "Since I am a prisoner of war that I was under duress, and that this treaty was not viable." He was sent to Cuba to keep him out of Mexico's affairs. In the next books, Santa Anna returns to power. He builds up a great army to continue the fight to reclaim Texas since she joined the Federal States against his wishes. His intent was to keep a hold on California, which has followed the example of Texas and became a republic. Next New Mexico becomes independent, so Santa Anna holds on for dear life as he wages all-out war against the Federal (United) States.

B

beau coups- (boo-COOS) French term: very much, a quantity, a great deal of something.

blacksmith: a man that works and forges iron into horseshoes, tools, and farming implements.

branch: Here it means the fork of a creek, stream, or river.

brave: a young, male American Indian warrior, or Native American warrior.

breeches: (or "britches.")- a slang word for "pants."

bull nettle- A green stinging plant, or weed. It was used before battle to be rubbed over the arms and legs of an Indian warrior to get him fighting mad and ready to endure pain. This plant was also dried and used in boiling water to make an astringent for wounds, used much like "witch hazel." The seeds taste like vanilla.

C

Californio's- settlers to California that rebelled against Mexico's rule much as Texas did. California was a republic that struggled as Texas did as a province of Mexico. The discovery of gold made a rush of settlers in 1849. California followed the example of Texas and became a republic, and it too became a bane to Mexico.

chaparral: Spanish word for a "road-runner." A large bird that chases down its prey of lizards, snakes, and insects. A sign of good luck for fine hunting for some Texas Indian tribes.

chiggers- deer fleas. Black land, and mesquite trees often have deer fleas that bite, and cause painful red sores that last for over a week. Sometimes it is so bad that people die from shock, or infection, if they do not treat it well.

Chitimacha- a Louisiana tribe that is part of the Caddo confederacy.

coal oil- oil from coal used as lamp fuel, and for soaking bad wounds.

Collin McKinney: A land surveyor. The architect and important signer of the Texas constitution. It was Collin's idea to make majority of counties in Texas as: "a 50 Miles Square with the county seat in the very center." (April 1846.) This was in case of Indian troubles, or if the army was needed to act in a hurry. Collin County was named after him, with the county seat named McKinney. Collin McKinney often disagreed with Sam Houston's ideas and actions. He often spoke out when he did.

Comanche: A great Indian nation composed of the Nacona, Wanderers, and Honey Gatherers. This tribe numbered greater than any other Texas tribe. They covered an area of West Texas called the Comancheria. Notable historical chiefs are Peta Nacona, and Quanah Parker, father, and son. (The son, Quanah, was born to a captured farm girl, Cynthia Ann Parker, captured after a Comanche raid on Parker's Fort in 1845. Quanah was a great, and wise peacemaker.)

Comancheria: The land belonging to the Comanche nations. It went north and west of Bird's Fort. It continued south all the way to the Rio Grande River. It was bigger and contained more people than all the settlements combined, and doubled.

Consultation: The 1836 meetings of the infant Texas Congress to make a valid Texas constitution.

contrary, or contraries: a group of people that live within a tribe that think, act, and dress opposite of what is considered normal. They served as an example to others on what not to do. They were tolerated because they had a different vision of the world, as they were crazy, or they were thought to have some sort of supernatural power.

corral: a fenced in area used to hold horses, or cattle.

council stick: a ceremonial stick wrapped in rawhide, and decorated with rabbit fur, beads, and charms. This stick was passed around in Indian councils to allow the speaker to talk without being interrupted. It would then be passed to the next person. If anyone interrupted the speaker, the stick would be used on the offender. This was a way to cut down on the internal strife by allowing the person to say their peace, and get it off their chest, keeping turmoil within the tribe to a minimum.

coup: (coo) the touching, or hitting of an enemy by a warrior, with a stick, or by a bow, or a horse hair quirt.

Sometimes the enemy was left unconscious, and their weapons, horses, and self-esteem would be taken. It was a big deal to brag about over the evening fire that you had crept up close enough to an enemy, and lived to talk about it to others.

coyote: Spanish word meaning "prairie wolf." A fierce animal for its size.

Cross Timbers- The northern part of the Trinity River forms three forks of the river: the Elm Fork, the Clear Fork, and the East Fork. The settlers called the river the Cross Timbers, as they resembled the shape of the Cross of Jesus. It was originally named this by the early Spanish explorers. This place had the best land for farming, and most had come here for that purpose: to own farmland of their very own without paying half their profits to the landowner. The Indians of this area called it "the old hunting grounds."

D

Deaf Smith- General Sam Houston's main scout. (Erasthmus Smith) He looked for a river route between the Sulphur, the Red, and Mississippi rivers, as the Mexican navy has many times blocked the boat routes in the Gulf of Mexico, between New Orleans, and Galveston.

Delephine- Andrew's first wife that was killed in an attack by robbers when they first came to Texas in 1836. Andrew was severely wounded, and he was almost dead when the Cherokee found him. She fought fiercely against the robbers, so much so that the Cherokee gave her a burial worthy of a brave warrior. She was uncommon, and she knew Andrew all her life. (Mr. Jeremy, their adopted father, stole them away from slave traders at Baton Rouge. His wife and child died in childbirth, and he could not stand to see children abused, or sold in bondage.) Many families of different races were sold into bondage as many people were in debt, in terrible Debtor's Prisons, unable to pay taxes, and debts, after the failed markets, and depression in the Federal States after the 1812 War. In those days whole families were in prison, or loaned out to work off their debts for 10 to 20 years, and longer! Laws changed to make it just for seven years to make it easier to get out of debt. This was several centuries before credit card companies come into being, otherwise we would all be in a prison these days! So please understand that many people were sold in bondage which included blacks, whites (English, Germans, French, Scots, Irish, and the like) whom were paying for their passage to America. Some Indians tribes, and individuals, were trying to buy back their traditional homelands as individual farms to re-establish their communities. This was common practice in those days, and it was a tragic fact of life.

Duellos- Greek word for "Slave." Also means "hard-working." A person with good skills.

dew cloths: curtains for the windows of a cabin. Also, the hides lining the inside a tee-pee to keep it insulated, and to draw the rain out of the sleeping/living area.

Dove Settlement- the settlement at Dove Branch, and the Lonesome Dove church/settlement. (Close to modern day Southlake, Texas.) This settlement allowed blacks, and Indians (Native Americans) to live there as it was also their settlement. All were welcome that were law abiding, and peaceful persons. A real and historical place that was the ideal place to farm and raise your family. This is not to be confused with a popular fictional story that "borrowed" the name for a story that does not related to most historical fact.

dog-trot: two cabins, or a cabin and a barn that are set up very close to each other with an overhanging roof that allows protection from the elements between the cabins. This allowed a covered work area in the heat or cold weather.

Dr. Jones- Doctor Anson Jones, a doctor that served at the San Jacinto battle.

He was the last president of the Texas republic.

E

East Fork: The East Fork of the Trinity River was used to bring goods from the Red River (and Mississippi) before there were roads that were passable in Texas. The Caddo and Cherokee used this river route for over 100 years before the settlers came. They fought each other for control of the river in 1804-1806, as iron, flint, furs, pelts, guns, and silver moved down this route since there were not many passable roads or trails in those days.

Empresarrio: Leader of legal land grants made in Texas by permission of the Mexican government. Moses Austin, Stephen F. Austin, Juan Seguin, Henri DeZavala, and later Henri Castro were Empresarrios. This was during the time that Texas was a Mexican state, and later a republic. (1824-1836.) These great men planned and settled Texas with their great vision.

E-OH-La: Cherokee word for "great wind." A cyclone, or tornado. A great windstorm.

escarpito: The French provided the Mexican army with a few of the new prototype of the modern shotgun. It fired brass rifle balls used to kill birds. This was the type of gun used on Sam Houston when he was wounded in the LEFT (tibia) ankle at San Jacinto. (April 21,1836.) *According to Sam Houston IV, Sam Houston's great-grandson, grandson of Temple Houston. He said, "It was Sam Houston's left ankle wounded, NOT the right leg as most paintings and references show." He then added the fact about the shotgun that fired brass rifle balls, which was a new type of gun for those days! He also added, "Sam Houston might have suffered from Diabetes, which is the reason why he suffered with his battle wounds for years. His wounds never healed well and he suffered terribly much all his life." This was from a phone call to the author held in June 2003.

F

farrier: a person that tends to horses by grooming them and filing down their hooves. This keeps a horse healthy and fit, and reduces the possibility that a good horse will go lame.

Federal States: the early name of the United States. In the days this book "happened" it was called the "Federal States." The "United States" was more a reference after the Civil War.

feather ceremony- a ceremony where young braves get a feather as a sign of achievement, and merit. It is much as when a soldier gets a merit stripe, or a raise in rank, or a medal for bravery. Young men between 15 and 22 "winters" old were taught hunting skills, fire making skills, making a shelter, and the use and making of weapons.

Federal States: The United States. This is the name that the United States of America was known by in the early days of its settlement. (The "United States" was more of a term more often used after the Civil War and Reconstruction when it was reunited after the internal strife.)

Fort Texas: March 27, 1846. American General Zachary Taylor took a prominent northern bank of the Red River to build an earthen, star-shaped fortress to keep the Mexican forces in check at the safe river crossing. Mexican General Mariano Arista started on May 3rd. This week long siege was to wreck the advances of

Texan reinforcements towards Mexico. The Mexican artillery from Matamoros fired cannon volleys to try to destroy the fort. Only two Texans died during the attack, which was surprising considering the length, and fierceness of the Mexican army's attack. It was also called "Fort Brown," by some people to honor one of the soldiers that died in that battle. He is all the same man that the town Brownsville is named after.

Free City: a settlement of free and escaped slaves that was close to Grapevine Springs and the Lonesome Dove settlement, in north Texas. The army and the Indians left them alone as they were peaceful, and farmed, and captured horses for the army, and they did not allow outlaws, or vagrants. The settlement was hidden in some hills among some cedars. The original settlement was in a limestone cave, northwest of Grapevine, Texas. It is now called "Sam Bass Cave," where that outlaw hid out, over 30 years later. Over 184 free slaves lived in Texas. Over 600 run-away slaves lived in early Texas. The local tribes hid them, and adopted many slaves. Andrew was adopted by the Cherokee tribe.

freedmen, or freemen: freed African slaves. Over 184 freedmen had come to Texas as a republic with the hopes of starting over, as Andrew had done. The army largely ignored Lamar's 1840 law that made freedmen forced to leave Texas if they had no legal reason to be here. Andrew had a legal manumission letter stated he was a freeman. He had additional land because he served honorably in the Texan army. Some freedmen lived among the Indians to trade and married among them, as the tribes could relate to their struggles.

funk- a depressed mood for a period of time.

G

gable-the forked part of the roof. A wooden rafter.

Grants, Land Grants: Second Class Head Rights, 1,280 acres for families, and 640 acres for single men after March 2, 1836. 640 additional acres went to men who fought in Texas battles. Land titles stopped for a brief period in November 1835 when it was feared settlers were coming undocumented and unregulated buying land at fifty cents per acre. This alarmed the army who had feared the newcomers would take all the good land.

Grapevine Springs: Grapevine, Texas. The site of the 1843 Great Council in which Sam Houston united the Red River Tribes allowing the new Peters' colonists to come here to settle. The author's hometown where his family lived for generations, some living there before it was a town, and before Texas was a state, or a republic. The Torian log cabin is a Texas Historical place, moved from its original site along Dove Creek to Grapevine Town Square on the Main Street.

Great Council: Council made up of the Red River Tribes: The Arapaho, the Delaware, the Biloxi, the Kick-a-Poo, the Ez-e-Nye, the Kiowa. The Wichita bands: the Tao-Va-Ya, Tawakoni, Tonkawa's, (and the main Wichita Band.) The Caddo: the Yoiuane, the Timber Hill, the Honey Grove, and related groups.) The Nadarka was a tribe that lived along the Red River from before historic times . The Great Council met September 28, 1843, at Bird's Fort, the point farthest west that Texas was settled at that time. The land west of Bird's Fort belonged to the Comanche. To the north, to the Red River, were the Kiowa, and Wichita nations. These tribes first met at Grapevine Springs close to present day Grapevine, Texas

gauchos- Spanish word for "cowboys." These are the "real deal" as far as cowboys are concerned. Their horsemanship, skill, and ability to train and break horses are unequalled.

gourd- a hollow fruit with a tough case, it grows on a vine. It was used for water, and food storage.

Goyens, William: A freed Black man that farmed, and traded horses with the east Texas Cherokee. He was the first to try to make a binding peace treaty between the Texans, and the Cherokee. Lamar made this effort impossible since he had control of the Texas Senate. William Goyens was an officer in the Texas' army, a first for a freed Black man in Texas.

grist- wheat, or corn is ground at a gristmill to make flour, or meal. The grist is the courser

part of the grinding that is often used for animal feed.

H

hand jack- a pump jack- used to pump ground water by hand. Indoor plumbing was unknown in those days and all water had to be hauled in buckets from a well or a stream. A hand jack would be a real timesaver and a wonderful help.

Hardin Runnels: the only person to run against Sam Houston, and beat him in his run for governor of Texas in 1848. Hardin Runnels made an 1848 law that "required freed slaves to take masters." This was a bad move for the governor as he caused a great deal of strife between blacks, whites, Indians, and Hispanics, as most fought to protect the rights of all people in Texas that were law abiding, and hard-working: as most were, or they would not be here long, or be tolerated in any settlement. In spite of what you may have read from other fictional sources: people coming to, and living in settlements were carefully regulated and protected by the army and the Texas Rangers.

harrow: A plowing platform on which a person stood while a team of horses pulled it across unbroken land. The platform had knife-like spikes that tore up the ground to make plowing easier.

hearth- a place where fire was made, and food was cooked there.

Houston, Sam: Twice the president of Texas, governor, head of the Texas army, and a representative of Texas to Congress. A true Texan in every sense.

I

Indians: "Native Americans" At the time of this story, the term "Indians" meant any native peoples living here in Texas and the Federal States. This book is written in terms used in the early days of Texas and the Federal States. (Andrew spoke in these terms.) So this book is written in Andrew's words, as he saw things in the 19ᵗʰ century perspective of a settler coming to Texas. "The term "Native American" was an unknown term in those days, so this reference does not apply here between these book covers as it would be awkward to speak this way in this particular forum. "Native American" is proper for today, to be totally "politically correct".

J

Jefferson: A town from which the steamboat brought important goods from the Red and Mississippi Rivers. All goods to the settlements came from here, and most modern roads in Texas owe their origins to Jefferson as the paths were cleared of trees to allow wagons to pass through. Indian trails were secured to travel there to get goods. Highway 380 is a good example of that going east and west. It was the old buffalo trail used by the Red River tribes. Many major highways were well-worn Indian trails, wagon trails, and traces.

johnny cakes: a pancakes cooked in lard. Cornbread. Sometime a pancake made of corn, or ground mesquite beans.

jujus- A small "apple-like" fruit that grows in parts of Louisiana. It is said to have been brought from Africa.

K

Kiowa: an ally of the Comanche. This tribe had its origins in the Rocky Mountains. It was pushed south to the Plains by the Cheyenne nation. The Kiowa moved about a great deal. (So much so that they did not make pottery.) Some Kiowa were war-like, but most were peaceable hunters and traders. The best-known chief of the Kiowa is Spotted Tail who watched over the settlers, and scared off hostile Indians. (And some bad settlers.) Chief Spotted Tail (Hawk) went out to find the settler's lost 3 year-old son in the middle of a fierce thunderstorm. He knew that if he waited too long that the boy's trail would be washed away and that the boy would perish all alone in the woods where bears and wolves were frequent inhabitants. Chief Spotted Tail lived close to Fort Buckner and McKinney. He watched over these areas like it was his own village. He died protecting these people from harm when smallpox hit the North Texas area after the Civil War. He tended to the sick, and became sick himself. He is one of many notable "Native Americans" that lived in Texas.

L

lagniappe- (pronounced "lag-Nap.") An unexpected gift. A nice present. A pleasant surprise.

lance- a highly decorated, ceremonial spear with a flint, or iron tip.

la trine: also latrine. A rest room, or out house as it was in those days. The latrine was a wooden shed built over a dug pit. Indoor plumbing was unknown in the 19th century.

La Crosse: (lacrosse) a sacred ballgame played by the Native American tribes before hunting and warfare. Often players suffered serious injury, such as broken bones, as it was an intense game that was often played on a field that was miles across between the goals. The elders would keep score, and maintained fairness, and tend to the injured players.

lean-to: (lean-two) A simple shelter put up in a hurry. You basically "leaned two boards (or planks) together." It was covered with a tarp that was tied down with rope to keep it from blowing away.

Louisiana Coffee: a stout coffee made three times stronger than regular coffee. Most farmers are so short on time that instead of drinking three cups of coffee they would drink one cup of exceptionally strong coffee. They used chicory to enhance the coffee that was so strong it would give you "goose bumps" if you were not use to drinking it.

M

ma`chu- an American Indian- fried corn dish made with onions, bell peppers, and tomatoes, (a Mexican discovery.)

mano: An Indian grindstone, oval and flat on both sides. Some have finger pits put into them by careful flaking, and hammering. Some of these grindstones were passed down from mother to daughter, making most of them quite old and worn from use. It is one of the most common Indian artifacts to find. It marks the place of a good campsite.

manumission: the act of freeing an indentured servant or slave. Often a person's debts were bought off by a wealthy person. The debtor had to work seven years before the debt was paid. Debtor's prisons in Andrew's day were full of people who could not pay their debts. It was a terrible place to be, for whole families were put in prison to be put to work at hard labor, for long hours in some terrible conditions. A legal letter was written to show that a debt was paid in full so that no one could make future claims against the debt. In this story Andrew and Delphine were children who were stolen from a slave auction by Mister Jeremy. His own children died at birth, along with his wife. He acted as their father and mentor. Mister Jeremy feared that someone might try to claim his children as slaves after his death. His will and manumission letter exhibit that Andrew and Delphine owned his property, his cabin and livestock because he considered them as his children, not slaves. They owed no debts so they owned everything free and clear. This is an example of the purpose of a manumission letter.

March 27th in Texas history: 1814-Sam Houston under the command of Andrew Jackson fights the British in Alabama, in the Battle of Horseshoe Bend, the decisive battle of the 1812 War. In 1836- The Goliad Massacre of the Texans that surrendered to Mexican troops. In 1846-the siege of Ft. Texas by Mexican forces along the Rio Grande.

mesquite tea: a pain reliever made from the boiled leaves of the mesquite tree.

me-te: The base from which grinding corn or mesquite beans takes place. It is a large flat rock, or, it is sometimes a wooden log, or tree stump.

Midway Camp- a campsite located between the Lonesome Dove Settlement, and Grapevine Springs. It was also the halfway point between Dallas, and Ft. Worth. (Then Bird's Fort which was the point that was settled the farthest west. Bird's Fort was a smaller fort a few miles east of present day Ft. Worth.)

milpas- Spanish for "cornfields." A large field of corn that can go on for many miles.

N

Nacogdoches- Sam Houston's home during the time of the early Texas settlement, and land grants. An ancient home of the Caddo nation in Texas.

newbie: slang for a new and unnamed baby.

O

Old Texians: The original early settlers of Texas. Some were Anglos, and some Mexican born.

P

parfletch: A leather pouch used for storage. A leather container that unfolds flat to place an object (usually meat) secured in the center to keep it cool and clean. The sides fold down, and it is tied secure keeping the contents dry, and secure. Meat tamales wrapped in corn shucks are an example of a Parfletch. Also "Parfletche."

par-lay- French "to speak." A chance to be understood and to speak freely without fear of harm or fear of death to the speaker. A forum for free speech.

Penne- Greek for "Poor Working" class. A person that works hard doing odd jobs to make ends meet. They are still living in poverty, but they are working two or more jobs. Also: a person with a serious work ethic.

Peters' Colonists- settlers from Englishman W.S. Peters' colony. An article written by the author concerning the Peters' colony follows this glossary.

pied- "spotted." A spotted cow (sook pied), a spotted horse, also: a person with freckles. (pied piper) Here it is used as a spotted buffalo, and its hide that was being fought over because it was a rare item.

pie keeper- a cabinet used for pie storage, to keep insects, heat, rain, and nosey people away.

Polk, James: President of the Federal States when Texas became the 28th state. Polk did more during his term as president than his predecessors as far as making life better. (He added the territories of Oregon/Washington state, New Mexico, and California.) He waged a continuing war with Mexico over the addition of Texas as a state. These other states were added after a peace treaty and a sum of ten million dollars. This addition of more territories to the Federal States is much like the acquisition of the 1803 Louisiana Purchase with France's Napoleon. This helped Mexico with their terrible war debts, and helped give them some compensation for their land losses. The additional states added to the Federal States, and Polk's manifest destiny to control the whole continent. It brought the slavery issue to the forefront as the slave states were fighting for control and power to push their authority to the newly acquired territories. The balance of power shifted each time a new state was added. This issue helped bring on the American Civil War in 1859.

potlatch: a meeting and trade time usually in the Spring and Summer seasons.

Pow-Wow: A big ceremonial dance held by American Indians. It usually occurs during the June 21st Summer Solstice celebration. The Rain Dance is held to bring the late summer rains.

The Jimson Weed Dance, called the "Crazy Dance." The single adults are matched up for future marriage. The Eagle Dance was held for blessing the earth, and the hunt.

puma- a mountain lion, or cougar. Andrew's Indian name given to him by the Cherokees.

Q
Qual-Li: or Qualls- The female leader of the Xensi warrior society. In the Caddo form of government women

held high places in their councils. Some women were head of the councils concerning matters of the hunt, also on the matters of warfare. Only the chief could challenge the outcome of their councils. Women sponsored great earthworks where terraces were built for fire temple structures, and ceremonial structures. Men moved hundreds of baskets of earth to build these terraces. Some men were designated hunters; some were farmers, some hunters, and some warriors. The Caddo have an ancient, ordered society. It worked well for them for thousands of years. Anyone with a "Qual, Quall" name, or "Qua" is a person of high stature and ranking in the tribe. The elder men of the tribe consulted the younger men of the tribe on the fine points on hunting, and dealing with the women of the tribe.

R

rasp: a file used for wood finishing, or filing down horses' hooves so a blacksmith can put iron shoes on them.

remuda: A nice sized group of horses ready to be traded.

ristas: a hundred or so peppers, onions, or garlic's are strung together on long strings where they hang from a peg, or nail in kitchens and doorways, and on doors.

They are also "a sign of good fortune," and they were thought to help ward off bad feelings and evil spirits. These are given as gifts many times to strangers, and this promotes good trade and positive feelings.

S

Santa Fe Trade: the area of Santa Fe, and the Santa Fe Trail was claimed by Texas. It was hoped that Texas could tap into that trade that had solid backing in silver, horses, and agriculture. It was hoped that some of the taxes put on goods could be circumvented to help pay the 10 million dollar plus war debts of Texas. It seems that Santa Fe did not want being obligated to pay taxes to a distant Texas, than Texas felt strained to pay taxes to a distant Mexico City. They fought against this as much as Texas did to Mexican rule. Sam Houston has tried to tap into this trade, as well as Mirabeau Lamar as the presidents of the Texas republic. They failed in this and this is what prompted Texas to be annexed to the Federal States to help make their government more stable with solid backing for their trade dollar. A bad trade dollar kept roads and schools from being built, or enough taxes to pay for the army.

San Jacinto: The battle that led to Texas Independence from Mexico on April 21, 1836. Also this is the land and place where a battle was fought. Andrew and Red Bird fought in this battle with Sam Houston.

Seguin, Juan: a great Tejano that escaped the Alamo siege to get help before the Mexicans could bring more reinforcements. He later left Texas to live in Mexico when he was accused of being disloyal and a traitor. He was devastated for he had given up all he had fought for to have the new settlers take it all away from him. He had been the first vice-president of Texas during the provisional government when David Burnett was the temporary president. Seguin is a great Texan who needs to be well remembered for his sacrifices to make Texas safe and independent.

siesta: (see-**ES**-ta) A tradition from Mexico and Latin American countries. During the hot part of the day people took a nap and rested until the afternoon cooled off and work could resume again. General Santa Anna was captured when he was caught with his guard down, with no sentries posted during the Battle of San Jacinto. He was caught later in the day, as he hid among the dead dressed as a private (soldier) hoping to escape in the night to safety. Andrew also saw the Mexican deserter as the captured Santa Anna dressed in rags to hide who he was.

Sook, or Sookie- a slang word for cow. So "sook-pied"
means it was a "spotted cow."

stand- used as a verb- to make secure- to fight unflinching,
unafraid, and bold.

Sugar Hill: Captain Y.B. Yeary of San Jacinto got his land
grant and opened a trading post northeast of present
day Farmersville, Texas. He was shot and killed trying
to break up a fight during a Christmas celebration
in 1848. Two brothers in their mid-twenties named
Glass were killed by friendly fire, being in the wrong
place at the wrong time. Sugar Hill got its name for
a time when wagons came from Jefferson with just
sugar and flour while the other wagons were delayed
by a storm and wagons that were bogged down. So
for about a week there was plenty of sugar and flour
but no coffee, or other staples until the other wagons
arrived. It was a long-standing joke for many years
and the name stuck for that trading post. The Sugar
Hill area is now a group of fine houses called Willow
Brook, outside of Farmersville, Texas.

sweat lodge: A ceremonial lodge used for cleansing rituals.

switch: A long wooden stick, or tree limb used as a tool to reach something.

T

TABOR: Texas Abolitionists Being Organized (for Rights.)

The name comes from the Bible, the Book of Judges, Chapter 4. Also the name of the many abolitionist supporters were called the Knights and Daughters of TABOR. Many Texan churches and citizens of different races supported this group as the acquisition of new territories: the question of spreading slavery was always in question.

tack- goods used for riding a horse: reigns, a rope lasso, a bit, and bridle, saddle, blankets, and such.

tare- an old English word, or term for a weed, or useless undergrowth.

Tejanos: Mexican born citizens of Texas. They were farmers and horsemen that rebelled against high taxation and joined the movement for Texas' Independence. Many of their sons were conscripted against their will for fight the Texans for the Mexican army. Their crops, and horses were taken without consideration of payment. This book celebrates the action of the Tejanos' fight against a well-trained Mexican army, outnumbered, against impossible odds. They joined the Texan settlers as they were all in the same boat, trying to make Texas a good, and safe place to live and make a living by farming. As new settlers came, some tried to make them out as villains, or traitors, as this was false. Texas Independence was achieved because of their fierce opposition to Santa Anna. They are true heroes, often unsung and forgotten in most history books, movies and commentaries.

Tejanos: (second definition) Mexicans that were loyal to the Texas cause. Many of the Tejanos were farmers that struggled in poverty due to paying high taxes to Mexico. Some were poor even though they had bountiful crops. They still suffered in poverty. This was their reason to fight against Mexico. Many of them had lost part of family, and some had lost all their family at Goliad, Zantacas, and related battles of the Alamo fortress. Also, members of the Consultation suffered losses of kin and went against the Mexican government to make a new Texan government.

Tejas: (Te haas') Spanish name for the friendly Caddo Indians. The name comes from the Caddo word

"Tey-Sha," or Friend! ("Tey-Shaw! Wha-she-knee Washita." Friend, save us from the enemy." The person hearing it repeats the same words, then it means, "save us from the outsiders.")

It is used as a test used by the Caddo as a "password" to see if strangers were enemies, or friendly traders. The "Crying Greeting" met strangers. This was to throw the strangers into confusion, so it would give time for the Caddo to figure if the stranger was a friendly trader, or a foe. The Tejas were the Yoiuane tribe. (Members of the Xensi warrior society.) Texas got its name from this tribe of Caddo Indians. Natchitoches, and Nacogdoches (Nack-A-Dish, and Nack-A-Doches.) These are two Caddo names that figure in Texas and Louisiana's history.

Telahqua-the new Cherokee capitol after the Trail of Tears-July 22, 1840 was the forced removal of the Cherokee from east Texas, to Indian Territory, which is in present day state of eastern Oklahoma. Chief Bowles, and Chief Mush were the principal chiefs if the Cherokee in east Texas. They died in battle protecting the tribe from the Texan army, under President Mirabeau Lamar's command. This was their "City of Refuge" where no one could bother them.

Texas Land and Emigration Company: W.S Peters of London, England, came to Louisville, Kentucky to make legal land grants to settle parts of Texas. These land grants were sponsored by United States President Andrew Jackson, a mentor of Sam Houston. These emigrants to Texas were called Peters' Colonists. This is how the Red River settlements came to be settled.

Texas Rangers- a well-trained group of men that acted as a proper militia on the Texan frontier. The idea for a group of men that were a citizen-soldier militia that were formed to capture outlaws, and renegades that preyed on the new settlements. (This idea of men who acted as a "go-between" of the citizens, and Texan soldiers was conceived by Stephen F. Austin. The idea was implemented by Sam Houston as president of Texas.) The Texas Rangers kept the peace to make living here a worthwhile experience. Outlaws were hunted down and expelled, or imprisoned. People came here to start a good place to live where crime and lawlessness was not tolerated for long.

Texican: the name that some early Texans were called before statehood in 1845.

tinja-(TEEN-ya) A covered well, or cistern. A well that was covered by a stone, or a piece of wood to keep the water cool from the sun and c lean from debris.

trace- a trail, or pathway. "Trammel's Trace: a pathway going from the Red River through Caddo country to the east Texas settlements.

travois: (tra-Voys) A dragging device made of green wood so that it will bend. It was pulled behind a horse carrying people, (or a slaughtered animal back to camp.) The horse pulls the "V" shaped wooden posts with the narrow part of the "V" on the horse's neck. Cross members of wood were added to secure the carried item.

Treaty of the Guadalupe-Hidalgo- The peace treaty that was to settle the Mexican War with the United States.

Treaty of Velasco: the 1836 peace treaty made of Texans to the Mexican government declaring Texas independent, and free from Mexican rule and taxation. The main reason that Texas rebelled from Mexico was over taxation without representation. Santa Anna was sent back to Mexico with the treaty proposal. It was argued by Mexicans that the treaty was not valid since Santa

Anna was a prisoner of war, and not free to negotiate a peace treaty.

U

V

varmints- animal, or person that is a pest, or troublesome. Some were four-legged, and some have two legs as in some outlaws.

vato: A Spanish slang word meaning "big boss" or "main man".

Velasco: Southern Texas port where Santa Anna, Sam Houston, Mecham Hunt, and James Pickney Henderson made a peace treaty to the Mexican government under Mexican general Santa Anna. Santa Anna later stated that he was a "prisoner of war" so he was not free to make a binding peace treaty.

W

wagoner- a carpenter that makes wagons, the chief mode of transportation, and movement of materials, people, and products in the 19th century.

Washington City-the earlier name of Washington, the District of Columbia.

Washington-on-the Brazos: The Consultation (the infant Texas congress) of delegates met for over a month during the weeks ending March 2,1836. The representatives of the Texas settlements met in dire cold, and under the stress of losing family in recent attacks made by Mexico. Also, Santa Anna had men out looking to capture them and destroy the Texan Rebellion as an example to others who would rebel against his rule. Washington-on- the- Brazos was also the temporary Texas capitol when Austin was under Mexican siege, and during the "Archive War" when Austin and Houston City were rivals over government documents, and over the rights to be the legal capitol of Texas.

Washitas: (Wah-She-Talls.) Non-Indians. A person that was not born, but "adopted as an American Indian." Also, a non-member of a certain tribe that trades with them. A good ally of the tribe. Andrew and Red Bird were considered "Washitas" to the Comanche, Kiowa, and Kick-a-Poo nations.

Waterloo: the original name of the town of Austin, Texas before it was changed to honor Stephen F. Austin, as the new state capitol.

wigwam- A shelter made of wooden poles, and posts, covered with animal skins. A tee-pee like structure used for shelter. A fire pit was dug in the center to make a smudge fire of green leaves, or cedar to keep mosquitoes out. Small stones were put on the floor where the floor would be warm, and weed free.

window lights: a slang term for "panes of window glass." Pronounced by some elder Texans as "winder lites." A slang word that was a popular description for "glass panes" in early Texas.

Winter Count: The first day of spring. March 20th, the Vernal Equinox. A birthday: Indian tribes deem that if you survived the terrible winter that you have made it to another Winter Count. Children born during the winter were held up and given the name that they would be known by. A good life is always a great reason to celebrate.

X

Xensi: (Zen-SEE.) An elite group of Caddo Warriors. They were fierce warriors. Well respected by the Red River tribes. Chief Bintah (Bent Tree) was a notable Xensi member of the Yoiuane Caddo. Some of their leaders were the elder women of the tribe. Qual-Li, or Qualls: A type of name that has the variation of "Qua," or "Quals" represents.)

Y

yard bird- slang word for a chicken, or chickens.

yellow roses: symbolizes death. "The Yellow Rose of Texas" was a song about the plot to defeat of Santa Anna's efforts by a female spy that found out about the troop movements of the Mexican forces which kept the members of the Texas government from being captured and put to death. It was a popular song among the African-American community, and it was picked up, popularized, and sang in popular plays, and in saloons frequented by soldiers.

Yoiuane- (Yo-AINE) It means the "River People." This band of Caddo Indians were called "the Tejas" (friendly) Indians lived along creeks and streams that flow along white rock, (Austin chalk) in north Texas.

Z

Zantacas: The mining town that refused to pay tribute, and higher taxes to Santa Anna, and the Mexican government. Santa Anna made an example of this town since he was in dire straights for tax money to pay his country's high war debts to France. Santa Anna ordered this town utterly destroyed, and the miners killed, to make an example of them to the rest of Texas.

This was the start of the Texan rebellion over paying higher taxes to Mexico. The next was at Anahuac, close to Galveston when unfair taxes were levied. The next rebellions were after the massacre at Goliad, then at San Antonio at the Alamo siege. A year before the Texans being massacred at the Alamo Mexican General Cos had taken refuge in the Alamo. He was captured and removed as a prisoner. This caused the ire of Santa Anna looking for revenge. Zantacas was one first catalyst for the Texan rebellion and the start of the fight for the Tejanos, and Texans for independence.

RED BIRD

MEDICINE MEN AND MODERN MEDICINE

Modern medicine could learn a few things from Native American medicine. Many of the medicines that we now use had their origin as plant extracts and poultices. Poultices are applied as an external method of drawing the poison, or foreign material out of a difficult wound. Today I will speak of a limited group of plants native to Texas, (and the southern states) that were used as medicine and useful remedies for serious and life threatening ailments. (I in no way encourage the readers to use some of these plants, for the exact potency and use was done by someone that had generations of instruction and advice on proper dosage.) The potency of plant extracts was well understood and the shaman (or medicine men) well understood these things from a lifetime of instruction. One was a great shaman that once lived in north Texas. He was a Cherokee man named Red Bird. He was also a sign-talker that spoke several languages. He used sign language so well that he was able to help negotiate the 1843 Great Council between nine different tribes. (The Red Bird Treaty) An area south of Dallas was named to honor him for his greatness and a great commitment to peace. Unfortunately over time he has been forgotten. His name lost to modern thinking and "modern" ways. Unfortunately most of our ailments have endured over time and these great people's wisdom has been forgotten. A shaman named San-See trained Red Bird. He was also a great healer and an elder in the Cherokee nation. He lived to be over one hundred and eight years old. He knew something unique in wisdom to prolong his life and the lives of others. These great people understood suffering and healing.

This is a short list of some of the plants and their use for healing. Modern medicine could benefit from some of these remedies. Used properly there would be "new cures."

1.) Dewberries, mulberries, and black berries were used as preservatives mixed with chopped meat to make pemmican. The citric acid from the berries did not allow bacteria to form readily in the summer heat. It also gave meat a good taste and was good for the diet and digestion.

2.) Sarsaparilla was a vine that grows wild. It was boiled and cooled for a healing drink for bad stomachs, and digestion. Root beers were made from various roots and kept in gourds for storage. Roots from the cattail reeds were used also.

3.)   Primrose was boiled as a tea and used as a laxative since it is poisonous, much like sienna; it purges the body of poisons and waste.

4.)   Foxglove was a plant used for heart attacks. It has digitalis, which would restart an ailing heart, and give relief from the terrible pain associated with strokes.

5.)   Dill weed was used for colic's and crying babies, for a tribe could not stand to have an unhappy child that might give away their hiding place. Sound carries for miles across the prairies.

6.)   Bull nettle was dried and then boiled to make a great antiseptic which rivals anything that can be found in modern stores. My grandmother had this remedy that she used often for serious cuts.

Green bull nettle was brushed over the arms and legs of warriors to test their bravery and push them past the pain of battle.

7.)   Garlic's and onions were used for fever and cold ailments.

8.) Sage was burned in bundles to promote healing. The original form of aromatherapy, for certain. Sage's scent promotes a calming and restful sleep for the suffering.

9.) Five Fingers, a stout vine was cut and saved much like bull nettle. This was used for small pox when it broke out in north Texas after the Civil War. Close to Fort Buckner (McKinney) lived Kiowa chief Spotted Tail Hawk. He used this to help his tribe, refusing it for himself since the grasshoppers had come and eaten most of the vines in the area that year. He died since he did not use this cure. Pieces of rawhide were soaked in a boiled solution of Five Fingers and then placed on the person affected with small pox to help with the infection and fever that followed. This is one cure that would be good to investigate for some possible future need.

10.) Puffball mushrooms (blanco kondos) were applied to knife and gunshot wounds to stop bleeding and allow healing. Spider webs were also used in this manner to help healing begin.

11.) Poke Sallet (Pol-Kay- Salid, "Big Root-Poison.") This was picked in early spring to be used as a "tonic" to purge the body of poisons that cause cancer and illness. This is an extremely toxic plant that was boiled two times, sometimes three times and the water poured off and then served with a few potatoes and onions to hide the terrible taste. It worked very well and after July it could not be picked at all when red lines appear on the stalk. The stalk was then cut back for next year for it is an annual plant. The red berries were used for war paint, and decoration. Modern winemakers used the red berries to make the wine red colored and more appealing to the eyes. The 3 foot long roots of this plant was used to make modern medicine during the Civil War when the North had a blockade of the Gulf of Mexico.

12.)   Honey-Honey was used as an antiseptic to seal cuts from germs and dirt.

13.)   Sumac-Sumac was brushed on arrow and bullet wounds or applied as a poultice to help draw out the foreign object as swelling was promoted to keep from digging the object out, causing the avoidance more infection and damage.

14.)   Sulphur was used as a medicine and for keeping chiggers and mosquitoes. People who drank from a well or spring that had sulphur in the water seldom had insect bites and some illnesses. It is a slight rotten egg smell, but once a person got used to it, it wasn't so terrible if you were thirsty.

This is a short list of a few plants and their use. There are hundreds that could be listed as a medicine man's knowledge took a lifetime to accumulate.

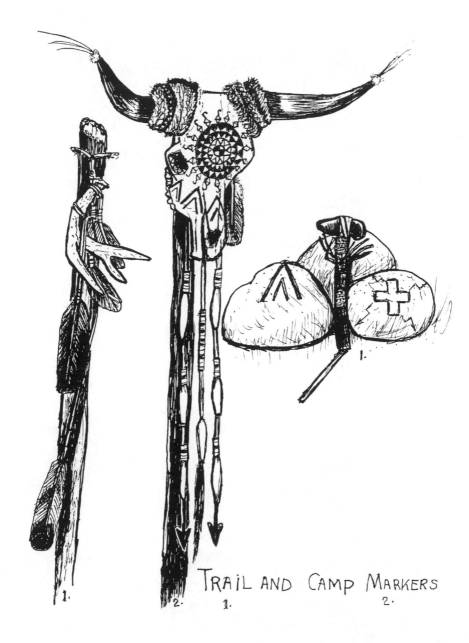

TRAIL AND CAMP MARKERS

1.   2.

WHY SHOULD WE REMEMBER OUR HISTORY?

The past is the foundation on which we build our future. That is why it is so important to understand and pass down our history to be understood and treasured by young and old alike. Our successes and failures give us a yardstick in which to measure our society as a whole. For without history there is no sense of direction as a starting point of reference in our lives. Our past is the only thing that we can be certain of in a struggling society.

Many people came to America to have a better life. Most families worked for a landowner many years to barely make ends meet. The same was true of Texas when it was a Mexican state in 1824. Many people in the Federal States were under the heavy burden of taxation. They faced going to a debtor's prisons, which is nothing like the luxurious prisons of today. The debtors were usually charged with high taxes and a large family to support. Judges usually offered the choice of, "going to prison, or going to Texas!" Texas was the lesser of two evils! My family came from Kentucky as Peters' Colonists for the chance to start over again fresh and new.

They came to a place called "the Cross Timbers" in the Red River Settlements in 1846. This was the historic "Lonesome Dove" settlement. (The true Lonesome Dove is located in Southlake, Texas.) My grandmother's family was named Torian and they were proud to be here considering the tough circumstances that they came from. Getting a land grant of their own to farm and do as they pleased was a dream come true!

It was the first real organized settlement and a church built as a focal point. In those days most people kept close in their faith and church met every third Saturday of the month. It was also the place that people got to meet and know each other. Many times your spouse was someone that your parents met at church and marriages were sometimes arranged that way. Neighbors that had adjoining farmland would double their land grants and water rights for farming. Sam Houston had made a Great Council of the Red River Tribes in 1843. Grapevine (Tah-Wah-Karro Creek or Tawakoni, as some said it, was the location.) There had been a three year Indian War here and Sam Houston as the new president, saw that there was a chance for peaceful councils to be made and a chance to resume new settlements that had been halted until there was some resolution between the tribes living here. My grandfather's family was from the Red River Tribes so Sam

Houston was someone that they respected well as a leader or "chief" of the Texans.

Many Indian tribes came from the northern Federal States to Texas as a last refuge. These were the Cherokee, the Delaware, the Arapaho, the Kick-A-Poo, and the Alabama and Coushatta nations to name a few. My grandfather's family was from the Cherokee and Choctaw nations. There were plentiful wild horses here so the tribes that lived here were quite fine horse traders and they were quite rich according to Indian standards. A person on foot did not fare well or live long so a good horse held a good value to trade when the dollar in Texas was "discounted" heavily. A discounted trade dollar in Texas was due to several reasons: republic President Mirabeau Lamar's Indian war and the building of Austin capitol. Also the printing of the "Red Backs" paper money due to huge Mexican War debts made the Texan trade less useful to outsiders. To people that we owed debts to in the Federal States. It was President John Tyler's push to make Texas the 28th state in late 1846, did our economic situation change for the better. (After two failed attempts.) We live in a tough time now, but what we have today is paradise compared to what terrible hardships our pioneer ancestors endured.

Joe L. Blevins

The Peters' Colony in Texas

What was the Peters' Colony? Why was it important to North Texas? The new exodus of pioneer families came to Texas as Peters' Colonists.

There were a number of reasons this happened: After the 1812 War many soldiers came back home to a troubling situation. Like many times after a war there were high unemployment, a bad economy due to war debts, and a drought covering much of the country. High taxes were levied against farmers whom were the largest proportion of the population. Most families were large in those days; and with a large family to support there were limited opportunities to change professions. What were their options? There were debtors' prisons where the whole family could go to work off their debts, but who could put their family through that ordeal? Judges would offer delinquent taxpayers few choices. They could "Go to jail, or Go to Texas!" The frontier of Texas was the lesser of two evils… People would put "GTT" on their cabin doors: "Gone to Texas."

In France they were finding themselves facing a civil war after Napoleon's defeat at Waterloo. England and Germany were also seeing a similar situation in their respective countries. So trying to find a way to ease the burdens of a large population, and ease the threat of a possible civil war was a big agenda item to be considered. Also Texas had its own problems with a struggling economy and trying to man its army and navy. The Texas government was looking for supporters to buy bonds, and sent immigrants to settle Texas. The Texas government wanted diversified settlements that would represent many interest, not just the interest of one country. The Texas trade dollar was discounted terribly because of the Texas Revolution.

The old Mexican EMPRESARIO system offered free land grants of 4,605 acres. The Peters' Colonists system in Texas offered every male 640 if married. 320 acres if a single man over 17 years old. Five or more women could join together to get a "single status" land grant in an effort to attract a husband. If a young man served in the army he would get 350 additional acres for serving 3 years' service as a citizen-soldier to protect the Texas' frontier. They were to put up a good cabin with stout fences. Also within a single settlement was provided to put up a section of land to put up a place of public religious worship.

For 5 years there was a great effort to avoid opening the Land Office. There was fear that the Texan army might rebel and leave their post, and older Spanish and settlers' land grants were threatened by the newcomers wanting to grab up all the good land. So there was more possible threat from internal strife than from the Mexican army, or Indian problems put together.

In late 1838, Sam Houston had proposed land grants from the French government since the French wished to buy Texan Wheat Bonds. General Sam Houston's Franco-Texian Project was failed in the Texan Congress. It was well know that France not only sponsored the Texans, for independence: France also sold arms, and supported Mexico as an effort to play both sides of the war to profit from the conflict by keeping things stirred up between both countries. (This is why Colonel Stephen F. Austin was in the Mexican prison those 8 weeks being called a spy. Austin was only the Texan diplomat to Mexico. He tried to capture the weapons cache to send to the struggling Texans.) Many persons hated this and they made it impossible to try to make any type of French proposal. The poor French farmers had no control over this.

But then there was fear of many persons coming to Texas unregulated, making claims to land that was possibly another's earlier land grant or claim.

The 1841 Peters' Colonists proposal came at a time that some viable proposal was needed. The Texan army would be in turmoil trying to fight the Mexican army, and trying to keep the settlers from fighting each other. So if the government could not support itself then the Texan government had bigger problems.

The original source of the Peters' Colony proposal is not known. It may have been proposed in Texas and the proposal put forth to the U.S. Congress by the American Phineas J. Johnson. Johnson went to Texas a number of times on business but he never moved here to live.

Since land was the biggest resource in Texas. Most land grants were free, but prime Government land along rivers could be sold for $1.50 per acre. With such a large area to choose from it was considered a bonanza to make millions of dollars in royalties to support a struggling Texan economy. There was a fear in the United (or Federal States) that Texas would **not** be settled by any single particular country, or any political group that would be a threat to them. These 20 Peters Colonists' petitioners were 11 Englishmen and 9 Americans were from Louisville, Kentucky. The Englishmen were: Daniel S. Carol, Alexander McRea, Roland Gibson, Robert Espie, William Oldmixon, Daniel Spillman, Robert Hume, John Salamon, William Byrne, Henry Richards, and Robert Stringer.

The Americans were: W.S Peters, John Bansamere, William Scott, Phineas J. Johnson, Timothy Cragg, and Samuel

Browning. The Americans were prominent businessmen of Jefferson County Kentucky. William Smalling Peters' name was the most prominent of the group of men and since his name headed the list. Since Peters lived in the United States and was born in England; he was thought the best choice to understand the different situations between England and America. Peters' family members held a piano making company in Kentucky, and a music publishing company in Cincinnati that gave his family some financial backing and influence in some political circles. His most notable published songwriter was Stephen Foster of "Oh Susanna," and "Camp Town Races." (And a few other popular songs.) But since W.S. Peters was in the promotional business and he was shrewd at it, it is respected that he was thought to be able to spot a good deal when he saw it.

Because of the distance between the English petitioners and the Americans, then Samuel Browning son-in-law of W.S. Peters went to Austin to sign the proposal to get the deal going before the interest was lost. Mirabeau Lamar the Second Elected President of Texas signed the proposal and they also signed the names of the others on their behalf of the 20 petitioners.

600 families were to be settled here total. 200 of the 600 families were to be settled here within a year. 400 were

to be settled within 2 years. The first petition failed because it was feared that trying to settle 600 families within a colony limits would not be possible to maintain and that there would not be enough "empty" land in a colony to allow for growth and roads, hunting and timber needs. (It was feared that the area would be settled so quickly the area would suffer from growth pains that could not dealt with in a timely fashion.) Also surveying an area of Texas that large required more time and money than they had planned. So there was quite an undertaking to get all the wheels in motion to make the details work. By July 1842 the third contract was in place was modified to be able to make boundaries extended and a timeline for a full survey was left open as it could be attempted or done. Trying to make an open prairie into a viable settlement is a logistic nightmare. Sam Houston made this extension possible by his interest and concern as the new Texas president. (Since the Texas constitution prohibited Lamar from running two terms in a row as president.) Lamar has made an Indian war with the Kiowa, and Comanche. Lamar exterminated the Cherokee from the piney woods of east Texas. It was up to Houston to address any Indian problems that would keep new settlements from forming in Texas. Fears and ignorance by the average settler slowed down the plans of any new interest in new land grants.

The English transferred their interest of the Peters' Colony to another group of Englishmen, since they were not involved as they should be. One particular Englishman was Sherman Converse took the reign of power and control on the English side of the contract. Something had to be done because it had to be maintained on both sides of the Atlantic for it to work properly.

The name of the Peters Colony was now a corporation that was called The Texas Agricultural, and Manufacturing Company. The next events as the company changed hands and faces as the new English "owners" try to negotiate in Texas, and New York as some slick business deals were happening. It would put some modern scam artists to shame. Many of the details were done under the table, as one Sherman Converse, an Englishman, was able to obtain the whole and full ownership of the original Peters Colony contract from the Louisville, Kentucky group, also! This Englishman Converse was a "Slick Willie" promoter that had more promises than potential.

December 3, 1842, because the new name was not attracting interest and it was losing money and support it returned as the Peters' Colony that it was formally known as. Sherman Converse made undocumented deals in Texas with both houses of Congress on January 20th 1842. Converse was given the power to make land policy that was unthinkable and unbelievable. The desperate situation in Texas called for some drastic measures as the government was about the split at the seams and the trade dollar was discounted 7 to 1 and then 10 to 1! There seemed no choice but to accept whatever carrot was tied to the stick, no matter how rotten it was! It seems that this desperation made common sense go out the window! Lamar's printing of the Red Dollars (paper money) made any choice was better than no choice. So Houston made the choice to leap before he looked. There was not any other choice for him to do!

Converse and D.J Carroll added 10 million additional acres to the contract. They had signed the names of interested parties on their behalf. The distance of 160 miles were added and the eastern and western boundaries. This latest contract made a dispute that lasted for years for so little of the details are actually documented. It did become the permanent basis for the Peters' Colonists. The total contract included over 16,000 Square miles!

January 4th 1844 Sherman Converse went back to London to try to establish more conservative partners as an effort to give his promotions of Texas land venture a greater credence. Europeans received him more casually than he had hoped for, but he was later received as the lead person and empresario of the venture after Texan diplomats Henry Daingerfield to the Hague, and Ashbel Smith in Paris promoted by their belief in Texas as a worthwhile investment.

Still other Texans had reservations such as Secretary of State, Dr. Anson Jones who felt that Sherman Converse was a crook and should be locked up and never should have been kept with such a free reign, as Converse had no reason to be trusted. So it was a matter of whom you ask what should have been done. The newspaper notices that the English had not taken Converse seriously and that the Americans had been duped and taken for a wild goose chase in business affairs. So Charles Mercer made a proclamation that Converse was a scoundrel and that he, Mercer, was taking the reign of the company. He sent Peters Colony secretary, and auctioneer E. B. ELY to try to save the company. In Texas, Ely and Mercer wrote Austin to the government to say that he was the new head of the company to say that Converse and their associates were no longer involved or be trusted. While Ely and Mercer were in Texas, Converse was trying to mend his broken ties with the Kentucky businessmen. He managed to do so being the slick operator he was. (This sounds like a crazy version of "The Musicman….") Converse was welcomed as the "Prodigal Son" as he tried to make his past indiscretions better. Converse went to Texas to find that all he had done in Kentucky was lost and now void.

It seems that the Americans had met with Sam Houston at Washington on the Brazos where the temporary government was being hosted. (Since Austin and Houston fought over the status of being the capitol of Texas, Washington on the Brazos was the safest place to be holding government because of the "Archive War." So this tells you that Texas was a crazy place to be as far as holding government was concerned... The Texas government had voted to nullify all the colonization contracts. Sam Houston vetoed the bill and put forth his own bill putting the Englishman Charles Mercer over the Peters' Colony project now called "The Texas Emigration and Land Company." The next day January 30th 1843 congress made a new law prohibiting Sam Houston as president to repeal or make any new laws concerning colonization of Texas. Houston's veto gave Mercer his own colony called the "Mercer Colony" or "The Texas Association," which was the reinstated "Fourth Contract." Converse and his associates lost all their rights. Mercer who was an abolitionist and "monolopolist" as he was called . He eventually lost his colony and claims to land there since he had not settled 250 colonists (families) by the contracted date. There were 197 families settled, and 184 single men. So not all families that had promised in their contract, had moved here as they should have.

(The author's family moved here at this time, to the Dove settlement, at the Cross Timbers of the Trinity River, close to Grapevine and Southlake Texas. This was the historic Lonesome Dove, the first settlement in north Texas.)

October 15th 1844

The Texas Emigration and Land Company was reformed by the company with new Louisville businessmen in tow. This is the time and place that the author's family came to Texas, (once all the dust settled.) They had planned to come sooner, but the turmoil and the scandal keep them from investing their time and money in the venture. Willis Stewart was the main person over the new venture along with W.S. Peters, and W.C. Peters, son of W.S.

A great many members of the earlier contracts had taken their lumps on the head. Many leaders of the Peters' Colonists "woke up" as far as seeing their earlier mistakes. So they were now valued members again in the remake of the old business venture. As always there was bickering within the ranks but it managed to stay afloat as a business venture. Some settlers came here and could not stand the hardships in Texas, and returned. I find that many persons missed their family that had stayed behind. This was the biggest concern for most that returned. Also coming here during the winter when corn was especially high priced to try to buy. It was the most desired food as it was easily stored and did not spoil easily as it is a basic, staple food.

In 1843 was a record wheat crop in Texas so that drew the farming interest here to raise some cabins and make their fortune here on their own land. The author Joe L. Blevins heard many stories about these days from both his grandparents that were part of the historic Lonesome Dove settlement in the Cross Timbers of the Trinity River: a great place to live and farm. It was just the place to start over with a clean slate.

The story just gets more twisted as there are land grants in the middle of Comanche lands where no white person could live without being short sighted as having a future there. So this intrusion into their lands to survey brought war parties in the regular settlements looking for revenge. This is what happened at Honey Creek in McKinney on Christmas Day, 1842. Also another attack was made on Dr. Ben Calder in February 1843 as he rode from McKinney to Ft. Inglish. (Dr. Calder had chopped down a bee tree that the local tribes of Kiowa's had thought the tree to be a sacred thing.) And the Muncey Family along Spring Creek on what is Highway 5 in Plano, Texas.

In April 1843 Sam Houston made a "Great Council" of the Red River Tribes so that unmolested settlements could be made in North Texas. So there are many different stories that come into play as we speak of the Peters Colonists.. This area of North Texas, Collin, Dallas, Denton, and Grayson counties were formed in 1846, the same year that Texas was the 28th state. At that time the colony was just in name only. Many had experienced difficulties in getting claims resolved, and few had proper deeds to attest to ownership. A year or so of controversy rocked different elements of the settlements as some local governments tried to tax properties that they had no right to without a proper survey of the boundaries. Those that lived on the boundaries were being taxed without know if they were actually a part of the area being taxed. They had no deeds to prove either way, so they were threatened to lose their lands that they had worked into a livable area of cabins and small farming communities. This was in Dallas area.

In May 1847 an Englishman named Henry O. Hedgecoxe was made the agent over the Peters Colonies and he kept surveyors from taken land that was already in dispute. But his arrogant attitude, British accent, and his less than tactful ways rubbed many people the wrong way, especially prominent citizens that were in error living on even numbered tracts that belonged to the government, and that they would have to move off land that had been developed by rivers. Others were issued half rights of 320 acres and so many would lose half of their land rights to another landowner. This British agent made many enemies as he sent out letters saying that the earlier Peters Colony contracts had voided their land interest and ownership, for the most parts. This conflict continued for about 7 years. In the end Mr. Hedgecoxe found himself hiding in a cornfield while many settlers were looking for him to give him a "neck tie party." Not a place to be honored in any *stretch* of the imagination. They did not have plans to celebrate like it was his birthday! Hedgecoxe went to an extreme to not properly do his job. He rubbed people the wrong way for much too long. It happens that way sometimes when you are dealing with so many people from so many different places, with different cultures where what is appropriate protocol one place is not setting well in another place. Many people were just hungry for land of their own, and they feared being left out in the rush to settle the frontier. The army feared all the land being grabbed up. There was a fear that the Texan army might leave its post to grab up their land, before "squatters" took up their choice land. (So the land office in Austin was many times closed by Sam Houston to avoid some real battles at the new state capitol.)

Mr. Hedgecoxe left Texas for "health reasons," for he had worn out his welcome. He did help organize the colonies,

Joe L. Blevins

but his motivation was to buy back properties with past due taxes as a hope to recoup on the future sales at some point when land values and demand for land increased.

In conclusion:

The Peters Colonists was a good idea that was handled badly over many failed contracts. In spite of the troubles it brought over 10,000 settlers to 17 counties of North Texas.

It was a time that Texas needed the land held to protect it from being overrun by Santa Anna.

The Peters' Colony was the largest Empresario colonization that was bigger than the Texan and Mexican empresario attempts combined. The Peters Colony and Texas Immigration and Land Company's efforts between 1841-1848 brought people coming to Texas for the next twenty years following the first contracts. It brought widely diversified groups of farmers, tradesmen, landowners, merchants, and artisans. This balance of different persons is what has made Texas great, for our differences are what make us strong, as a state, and a country.